# INITIATION INTO CANDOMBLÉ

INTRODUCTION TO AFRICAN-BRAZILIAN RELIGION

# INITIATION INTO CANDOMBLÉ

## INTRODUCTION TO AFRICAN-BRAZILIAN RELIGION

ZECA LIGIÉRO

*Translated by*
EMMA SYMES

DIASPORIC AFRICA PRESS

This book is a publication of

DIASPORIC AFRICA PRESS
NEW YORK | WWW.DAFRICAPRESS.COM

Copyright © 2014 Diasporic Africa Press, Inc.

All rights reserved. No part of this publication may be reproduced or distributed in any form or by any means, or stored in a database or retrieval system, without the prior written permission of the publisher.

ISBN-13 978-1-937306-29-8
Library of Congress Control Number: 2014938391

## CONTENTS

*Prefatory Note* — i
*Foreword* — v
*Old and New* — ix

**PART I: RESISTANCE OF A CULTURE** — 1
The Presence of African Knowledge in the Americas — 3
A Brief History of Candomblé in Brazil — 15
The Candomblé of Our Everyday Life — 23

**PART II: THE RELIGION OF THE ORIXÁS** — 29
The Axé: Colors and Forms — 31
Yorùbá Cosmogony — 35
The Orixás and Nature — 43
The Orixás and Their Archetypes — 47
Exu/Elégua: Orixá of Directions in Space and Time — 51
Ogum/Ogun: Orixá of Iron and War — 55
Oxóssi: King of Tropical Forests — 57
Iroko: A Tree Orixá — 59
Ossâim/Òsanyìn: Orixá of Wild Leaves — 61
Omolu-Obaluiê: Orixá of Illnesses and Cures — 65
Oxumaré/Òsùmàrè: The Rainbow Snake — 69
Nanã Buruku (Nana Buluku):
Great Mother of the Marshes — 71
Shango/Xangô: Orixá of Justice — 75
Iansã/Oya: Lady of the Wind and Storms — 77
Oxum/Oshun: Queen of the Spring Waters — 79
Iemanjá/Yemanjá: Queen of the Sea Waters — 81
Oxalá (Oshalá)/Obàtálá: The Creator of Human Beings — 85
Other Orixás and Entities — 89

PART III: THE DIVINATION SYSTEM OF IFÁ  99
  The Tradition of Ifá  101
  From Ifá to Jogo de Búzios  105
  Dafa: Consulting the Divination System of Ifá  107

PART IV: THE RITUAL:
THE ORIXÁS DRINK, EAT, AND DANCE  117
  Trance and Initiation  119
  Sacred Spaces of Candomblé  129
  Religion, Life, and Art  133
  New and Old Paths  137

  *Selected Bibliography*  141
  *Notes*  145
  *Index*  149

## PREFATORY NOTE

It is exactly twenty years since I published the first edition of this book in Brazil. When writing the book, in addition to interviews and direct contact with some of the priests and priestesses of Candomblé, I used the resources of a relatively small library belonging to the acclaimed studies of Afro-Brazilian cultures. Those studies ranged from Nina Rodrigues to Edison Carneiro, as well as French researchers Pierre Verger and Roger Bastide and two North Americans, Donald Piersen and Ruth Landes. In my initial research, a problem that inhibited my investigations was not only finding sources in the context of the times, but rather, in my fascination with the Yorùbá tradition, this led me to believe that their foundations were the only origins of Candomblé.

Today, we have more access to thorough investigations and many more facts at our disposal, such as anthropologist Luis Nicolau Parés, who demonstrates clearly the Jeje (Gêgê) form and origins of Candomblé. Parés's work provided further insights beyond the pioneering studies made in this area by Vivaldo Costa Lima and João José Reis (of whom I, unfortunately, did not have access before the first edition of my book in 1993). In the course of his research, Parés recognized an even more remote origin, about which there are still very few studies—the ancient *calundus* of Congo-Angola origin. It is a fact that in recent years the number of anthropologists, made up of journalists and curious people investigating the *terreiro* (sacred space) culture of Candomblé, has grown enormously. The ancient oral tradition of Candomblé is spreading across the whole of Brazil, in certain countries in the Americas as well as in Europe. In today's context it is being shared by a vast bibliography, which includes the popular magazines sold on newsstands, Internet sites, and to the point of a virtual consultation with a traditional Ifá divination system (*jogo de búzios*, or cowrie shells divination in Brazil) so that anyone can find out their *Orixá da cabeça*. (*Orixá da cabeça* or "Orisha of the head" refers to the principal divinity or Orisha that guides the "head" or *ori* of each person.)

Another key aspect, which has advanced my personal understanding of Candomblé since the first publication of this book, is in how my own study and practice have progressed after taking my first steps as a devotee to this religion. By now, I have completed fourteen years of religious confirmation, under the post of Mogba Sango in the Omiojuaro house of Candomblé of Miguel Couto, Rio de Janerio, led by Mãe Beata de Iemanjá and Bebé Egbé Adailton Moreira Costa. When invited to create a new edition of my book for the Rio de Janeiro publishing house *Pallas Editora*, I saw it as an obligation to review the original, to be able to examine more accurately many of my initial concepts, seeking to develop some of the historical aspects and the true symbolism of Candomblé. I trust that this revision serves to prove how with time, new research and reflections, and everyday experiences within the Casa de Santo, have seasoned my words. On the other hand, as the book continues to meet with success after so many years, arousing the interest of both academic researchers and the public, suggesting it must still be very much alive, and so there is no need for a complete rewrite for this English edition.

My brief visit to the region of Gulf of Benin in 2011 allowed me to watch a Festival of Black Divinities in Togo, and was a true immersion into the Jeje and relative worlds. Their diverse religious practice associated with the Voduns left me certain that they shared a great kinship with the religion of Candomblé in Brazil. The circular dances, the performances in a trance—or if not, in processions—the offerings, their objects, the use of "guias" (necklace made of *missangas* or glass beads) that indicate the colors of divinities, the turbans, and the hierarchical organization, all transported me to the houses of Bahian or Carioca Candomblé, even though they were venerating Voduns instead of the Orixá (Yorùbá: Òrìṣà; English: Orisha).

When I wrote the book in the early 1990s, I imagined Africa as a mythological continent, with a very old reference perhaps reminiscent of the prints of colonial exhibitions in English or (principally) French versions, influenced perhaps by the beautiful photos in black and white of Pierre Verger taken in the forties and fifties. In my imagined Africa, the original inhabitants maintained their cultures' purity, devoted to their ancestors and their true, unaltered habits. When I entered into contact with Candomblé, I came to perceive it as a restoration of an African life and a faithful continuation of an African religion in Brazil; such as in the case of the predominant Yorùbá tradition (in present-day Nigeria) influenced by the main studies of Afro-Brazilian culture of the times. Today, it is possible to make a more complete evaluation, and understand Candomblé not just as the continuation of a single tradition but rather as a multi-cultural creation developed on Bahian soil. Candomblé is the fruit of the harvest of diverse groups of many localities and African origins, whose religions, in their indigenous sense, already lived through a long process of coexistence and exchanges venerating various divinities in one single space.

# FOREWORD

*Gisèle Omindarewa Cossard*

When slave ships spilled out their African cargo onto the coasts of the Americas at the start of the sixteenth century, the white colonizers separated them, auctioning men, women and children. For the African captives there were no more couples, there were no more families, and there was no more village community. All that remained was despair.

Some, incapable of supporting such hardship, were left to die. Those who survived guarded in their hearts the memories of their indigenous land. However, any kind of regrouping was impossible in the large farmlands. At the start of the nineteenth century, in urban centers, the condition of certain captives began to be less harsh, and some managed to gain their freedom, either by combining forces with their companions, or by the charity of more benevolent slaveholders. Already the Africans were gaining certain autonomy, and over time they multiplied—their numbers born out of intercourse between the male slaveholders and the enslaved women. Soon, there appeared the great African captains sailing to the western African coast at the start of the commercial era, building for themselves a new community wherein ancient traditions were maintained, organizing for themselves authentic African religious centers.

Once again, the supernatural world received homage from its children:

*Mojuba orun* (Sky, I bend to you)

*Mojuba ile* (Earth, I bend to you)

*Mojuba ewe* (Leaves, I bend to you)

*Mojuba omi* (Water, I bend to you)

Once again, the divinities were present amongst their followers. Once again, the invisible world, which rules humankind, was accessible.

"Yatunde," the mother returns. Mother Africa, hot as a tropical night, majestic in her procession of divinities which surge out from the darkness, forces of nature, water, sea, mud, lightning, wind and thunder, forces which help us evolve and regenerate us.

The drums sound and the divinities, happy, dance, dance to the ancient myths, dance to the fire and its fury, dance to the freshness of the crystal waterfalls, dance to the wave that brakes on the beach, dance to the creation of the World...

And the divine blessing scattered about the humans:

*Ogum ka ji ré* (Ogun, that our awakening be in happiness)

*Oba ka ji ré* (Shango, that our awakening be in happiness)

*Osun ka ji ré* (Oshun, that our awakening be in happiness)

*Nji owo ni ka ji* (that, in our awakening, we encounter money)

*Nji aya ni ka ji* (that, in our awakening, we encounter women)

> *Nji omo ni ka ji* (that, in our awakening,
> we encounter children)
>
> *Ki a ma dide iku* (that we do not wake
> up to encounter death)
>
> *Ki a ma dide arun* (that we do not wake
> up to encounter sickness)
>
> *Ki a ma dide ejo* (that we do not wake
> up to encounter fights)
>
> *Ki a ma dide ofo* (that we do not wake
> up to encounter losses)[1]

It is this faith, admirable, so powerful that it resisted the worst adversities, revealing for us all an incomparable example.

## OLD AND NEW

Candomblé is an ancient religion that today still has many followers throughout Brazil. However, despite the popularity of Candomblé, many people still confuse the religion with a cult, or perceive it as part of other religions, such as Spiritualism, Umbandaism, or even non-orthodox Catholicism. Candomblé is an independent religion with a true philosophical base, and its own mysteries, beliefs, and rituals.

Many people receive an opportunity to visit a *terreiro*[2] at some point in their lives, even if it is just a quick visit. Some stay for good, not because of the "miracles" that can occur within, but rather because they discover the ethical principles that this ancient spirituality brought from its African ancestors. They also discover the fascinating beauty and mystery of the religion's divinities—from Orixá to the Voduns—and of the Nkisi (pl. Minkisi; divine powers in Candomblé of Congo-Angolan origin). So, little by little, people come to experiment, deepening their own knowledge of Candomblé and come to understand how a religion so old can still respond to contemporary issues: Who are we? What do we want? How can we live alongside the forces living in nature wherein the true temple where the divinities of Candomblé reside?

As we have entered a new millennium, we can feel pressured to depart from ancient wisdom brought from the African people. It is important to remember, however, that even under centuries of slavery and decades of political persecution, Candomblé secured for its believers the ability to preserve their independence of spirit, the full process of individualism, and the ability to connect with the forces of nature. In the passing of time, wherein we feel poisoned by the aversions and pressures of a world increasingly artificial and inhuman, it is time to look towards a knowledge which has always been on our side—Candomblé.

## A NOTE ON TERMINOLOGY

In this book, the terms "Orixá" (Brazilian Portuguese) and "Orisha" (English), which are variants of the Yorùbá term "Òrìṣa," are used interchangeably. The same is true for other Yorùbá cultural/spiritual concepts, such as àṣẹ (axé), as well as the names of the Orishas. The "gender" of the Orishas, and the divine forces above them (e.g., Olódúmaré), are used only metaphorically to indicate relationships amongst them and to talk about their roles and activities in human terms (.e.g, s/he, father/mother, son/daughter, wife/husband). These divine forces of nature, though at times depicted anthropometrically, are not human, but humans need to have a cognitively way to wrap their minds around their presence and utility. Finally, the Yorùbá language does not really make clear "gender" distinctions, especially of non-human forces, but English and Portuguese—the respective destination and source languages of this translated text—do.

# PART I

# RESISTANCE OF A CULTURE

## THE PRESENCE OF AFRICAN KNOWLEDGE IN THE AMERICAS

The Egyptians left us their myths stored in the pyramids of the deserts, the Greeks in the expertise of their sculptures and their theatre. In contrast, the Yorùbá saw their ancient records partially destroyed during successive internal wars—damage compounded by humidity in the tropical forests, looting by invaders, and slavery. However, a visit to modern-day Egypt would reveal that, aside from tour guides and students, nobody speaks anymore of the divinities Isis and Osiris. In contemporary Athens, Dionysus and Apollo, outside the museums, are names of restaurants and hotels. These two traditions are studied and catalogued as Western cultural heritage sites but they are no longer exercised as faiths. However, in Lagos, as in Salvador, Havana, and even New York, the Orixás such as Xango/Shango, Exu/Eshu, and Ogum/Ogun, among other Yorùbá divinities who are all almost as old as the Egyptian and Greek divinities, are still venerated.

Why does the tradition of the Orixás penetrate so strongly in both Africa and the Americas, despite having suffered so much persecution during European colonization? What is the reason for this incredible resistance?

First, we must turn to the Yorùbá society in Africa before the process of transatlantic slaving. Robert Farris Thompson, in the opening of his book *Flash of the Spirit*, poses an interesting idea with respect to the Yorùbá world. He speaks about the first vision of the city of Abeokuta by American missionary R. H. Stone, in the middle of the nineteenth century:

> What I saw disabused my mind of many errors in regard to...Africa. The city extends along the back of Ogun for nearly six miles and has a population approximately 200,000.... [I]nstead of being lazy, naked captive individuals, living on spontaneous productions of the earth, they were dressed and were industrious...[providing] everything that their physical comfort required. The men are builders, blacksmiths, iron-smelters, carpenters, calabash-carvers, weavers, basket-makers, hat-makers, mat-makers, traders, barbers, tanners, tailors, farmers, and workers in leather and morocco.... [T]hey made razors, swords, knives, hoes, billhooks, axes, arrow-heads, stirrups...[W]omen...most diligently follow the pursuits which custom has allotted to them. They spin, weave, trade, cook and dye cotton fabrics, they also make soap, dyes, palm oil, nut-oil, all the indigenous earthenware, and many other things used in the country.[3]

In short, the Yorùbá civilization had one of the most developed urban communities of black Africa. The ancient Yorùbá city dates back to the Middle Ages, between the twelfth and thirteenth centuries, when the sacred city of Ile-Ife boiled with an artistic force that would later provoke true amazement in the West. The sculptors of Ile-Ife were producing splendid works of art in terracotta and bronze; however, nothing compared in quality to that which was being produced in Europe during this time. The first missionaries who came to the city of Abeokuta in 1840 were astonished not only with the artistic production, but with the prestige the sculptors were given and their leadership within the community.

Something that was noted only later in time was the conscience of beauty, interior grandeur and elegance that was manifested in the works of Yorùbá art, amalgamated within the principal religions found in the life of the Yorùbá citizens. John Mason, a *babalawo* in New York, gave us an excellent definition of the concept of "art" for the Yorùbá:

> The Yorùbá use the word *Ogbon* to mean
> art, intelligence, cunning, wisdom, ingenuity,
> skillfulness, wit and invention. This idea coupled
> with the terms *Iton* for tale or history and *Ton*
> for diaspora, to propagate, to investigate, to
> shine, and to trick helps us to understand that
> for the Yorùbá, art is the propagation and
> investigation of wisdom. It is meant to shine, be
> seen, be heard, to trick and cause a double-take
> of the signified, a reinvestigation. Art is supposed
> to *Ru*, carry you, *Ru*, stir things up, incite you;
> *Ru*, move you to be either angry or sad. By its
> very definition Yorùbá art is meant to travel,
> spreading the news about all things sacred and
> mundane. All art begins with Divinity, the Ideal.[4]

The artistic peak of the Yorùbá civilization during the Middle Ages continued during its urban development until the middle of the nineteenth century. The location of its principal cities and their distances from the coast protected the Yorùbá people from the trafficking of captives ran by the Europeans at the start of the sixteenth century (there was also a slave trade run by the Arabs in Africa since the seventh century). However, the subsequent wars and expansion of the kingdom of Oyo, which subjugated other regions, resulted in the growth of slavery within the region. Together with the politics necessitated by war, a goal emerged: immediately turning new prisoners into captive individuals. The constant siege by Europeans and the incentive to traffic prisoners of war in exchange for necessary goods ended up also transforming the Yorùbá kingdom and the inhabitants of neighboring regions, including the lands of what is today Togo and the Republic of Benin, into a slave mill.

By considering human trafficking from Africa to Brazil, we can form an idea of how the arrival of African people contributed to the formation of Candomblé. Candomblé was composed not only by the Yorùbá, who came initially from present-day Nigeria and whom were generically called Nagô in Brazil, but also the Jeje (Gêgê), which are considered the founders or the first *nações* (nations) of Candomblé and whom spoke Gbe languages such as Fon, Ewe, and Aja. The Congo and the Angola Candomblés have been known for a long time and which represent the most distant links with the African motherland.

In 1538, the first African captives were brought to Brazil by European ships. It was the first human cargo that they notably bought; it initiated nearly four centuries of slave importation. In spite of their being but one larger denomination of "Africans," the captives were from many different cultural groups, and originated from different African regions. Generically, they were classified into two principal groups: the Bantu, corresponding to those from Congo, Angola, and Mozambique; and the Sudanese, including the Yorùbá, Jeje, and Hausa. Originally, the trafficking went in the direction of Salvador, the old capital of Brazil, and then to the cities of Recife, Salvador, and São Luis, after which were less official, clandestine journeys to other less known ports. Transatlantic slaving between Africa and Brazil can be understood in waves or cycles of migration:

1. The Guinea cycle in the second half of the sixteenth century.

2. The Angola and Congo cycles, in the seventeenth century, continuing in small waves until the end of trafficking in 1888.

3. The cycle of the Mina coast (that is, from the Volta river to Cotonou), in the first three quarters of the eighteenth century.

4. The cycle of the Bight of Benin, between 1770 and 1850; this was prevalent up until the period of clandestine trafficking.[5]

The two last cycles are particularly important for our story. In the Mina coast cycle, the commerce in captive individuals was intensified by the kingdom of Dahomey (Jeje) alongside a tax imposed on the kingdom of Oyo, the Yorùbá capital, which had a fundamental role in the trafficking of Africans. In this period, there were a great number of African provinces in the regions of present-day Ghana, Togo, and Benin, from where captives principally arrived in the cities of Salvador and São Luis of Maranhão. In the fourth and last cycle, we see that this mass transport of Yorùbá people to Salvador, which continued—together with the new capital Rio de Janeiro that received other people besides the Yorùbá—to be one of the principal ports of entrance for African captives.

The mass arrival of the Jeje people (Fon, Ewe, and Aja) and the Yorùbá or Nagô was a reason for their strong influence on Bahia's cultural life. If the Jeje developed the first central urban religions brought from the African continent, these along with the arrival of the Yorùbá people gained new shape and in many ways a new language. The Yorùbá also brought with them their knowledge and great capacity for political articulation. Whilst the religious life of the Jeje is organized around their divinities called Voduns, which simultaneously represent the forces of nature and the ancestral world, the Yorùbá people are organized around their divinities called Orixás. They have a divination system in common (Afa for the Jeje; Ifá for the Yorùbá) for a single divinity (Ọ̀rúnmìlà) and which speaks through the manipulation of shells (*dida owo*), known in Brazil as *o jogo de búzios* (the "game" of cowrie shells divination) performed by the special priest called *babalawo* (male priest of Ifá). After consulting the divination system, the devotee should make some kind of offering or sacrifice in a specific ritual to change the fate of things and prepare a healthy and steady new path. There are many common points between these religions, which in Brazil generated a specific type of Candomblé called Jeje-Nagô or Nagô-Vodun.

Factors that catalyzed the cultural resistance and renewal in Brazilian lands included the considerable presence of prisoners of war originating from high social classes, sacrifices made to preserve traditional values, and the perpetuation of religious rule. This preservation of the religious customs brought from Yorùbá lands to Brazil helped retain a great kinship with the two neighbors on the ancient Mina coast. It is also important to emphasize the differences between the dates of emigration for the majority of Yorùbá people to Brazil, in the beginning of 1830, and the fall of the ancient city of Oyo, the capital of the Yorùbá kingdom, conquered by the Fulani in 1835.

The Yorùbá people met their "enemies" in Salvador. Those who had ruled for centuries—Jeje, Hausa, Asante, Fulani, among others—now suffered considerable hardships. Many who had arrived in Salvador from the West African coast already converted to Islam and were known in Brazil as Malês (from Yorùbá *imale*). The Jeje and Yorùbá were the last important cultural groups to arrive, and met a great number of Congo-Angolans and their first- and second-generation descendants. With the exception of the *malês* (African Muslims) of diverse cultures who spoke Arabic, and who preached the teachings of the Qur'an, a great majority of the captives had little instruction; and many of those were already assimilated to the predominant Catholic culture while in Africa. Nevertheless, many also chose to continue practicing some aspects of Islam or Christianity, seeing no incompatibility between them. It is important to note how limited education was among the population of tradesmen. We must separate this from the fact that many of the Jeje and Yorùbá brought to Brazil skills such as blacksmithing, masonry, gem carving, and gold mining; notable also was their work with leather, steel, and livestock.

Already during this time, there existed resistive religious groups who continued to practice their indigenous African religions despite obligatory Catholicism. "Batuque" was a generic name given to the first religious groups who performed rituals or festive celebrations. A more specific term for the religion was *calundu*, which was of Congo and Angola origins. In Brazil during the seventeenth and eighteenth centuries, the word "calundu" was associated with the practices of African *curandeirisimo* (traditional African or Amerindian medicine) which involve a trance during a celebratory ritual for the ancestors, the process of turning water to wine, and the use of medicinal herbs. The term "calundu" derives from the Kimbundu word *kilundo*, which signifies the possession of somebody by a spirit. Naturally, the *curandeiros* that practiced *calundu* exercised great influence within the African community, since they were considered the religious leaders. Many of them also passed on the knowledge acquired by the indigenous and even Europeans, passing the practice of their medicine between those of few means. Around the work of these *curandeiros* the first Candomblés were born—as well as the true origin of the word, which is not found in the languages of the Jeje (Fon, Ewe, Aja), Yorùbá, or even Congo-Angola. Similar words include *ka-n-don-id-e* or *ka-n-domb-ed-e*, or more frequently used, *ka-n-domb-el-e*, which is the *ação de orar* (act of praying), a substantive derivation from *ku-dom-da* or *kulomba*: to pray, to hail, or to invoke. Candomblé signifies adoration, praise and invocation; and, as an extension of this, a place where ceremonies are realized.

It is interesting to note that the leadership of monotheistic religions such as Christianity and Islam, which were born in the deserts of the Middle East, supported slave merchants pronouncing through their religion the approval of trafficking of captive individuals. In the case of the rise of Islam, in the seventh century, the situation of captive individuals in the Arabian Peninsula was deplorable. In his influential book, *Slaves in the Lands of Islam*, Malek Chebel relates to us: "The Qur'an would want to end slavery, decreed a concretely policy of emancipation by Abu Bakr (died in 634), second caliph, who devoted his personal fortune to the emancipation of slaves. However, this was partly overturned by Omar (581-644), third caliph of Islam and his immediate successor. Islam has enacted a timid policy, without real constraints for the merchants of captive individuals, slave traders and their sponsors."[6]

The author provides a detailed analysis of the Qur'anic interpretation performed by Arab scholars in support of slave trafficking, thus transforming the phenomenon of slavery as part of the acceptance of the Islamic faith. During the new Islamic empire that formed after the death of the Mohammed in the year 632, the scholars of the Qur'an believed that the empire was bound to convert all people to Islam. Those who remained unfaithful could therefore be made captive individuals without pity. The captive individuals that converted to Islam could be saved, with only minor punishments given to those who denied the words of the Mohammed. The Arab expansion into African lands concurrently increased slave trafficking, bringing to the slave merchants centuries of an enslaved African population. Affected regions included North Africa and penetrating into the Sahara, in the direction of the central regions, reaching as far as cities such as Gao and Timbuctu in the ancient region of Mali; likewise, it extended south and east, to Zanzibar, and penetrating the lands neighboring the coast such as Nubia, Sudan, Somalia, and Ethiopia.

The exportation of black captives fed not only the European market (Cordoba, Barcelona, Geneva, Naples, and Venice), but all of the Middle East, as well as advancing toward Constantinople (Istanbul) and distant cities within Asia such as Bukhara (Uzbekistan) and Kashgar (China). Securing the old "Silk Road," all of these areas crossed three continents that made up part of the old Islamic Empire. The famous "Zanj" rebellion that occurred near the city of Basra, in the south of Iraq, and would have taken place during a period of approximately fifteen years (869–883), indicates the enormous quantity of enslaved Africans transported to this region. The initial riots culminated in the rebellion of more than 500,000 captives that were imported by the Muslim Caliphate, costing tens of thousands of lives in lower Iraq.

With Spanish and Portuguese explorers' discoveries, the slave market would expand west and south across Africa, and attain principally the cities and empires located on the Atlantic coast, driven forward by new markets and political support in France, Holland, and England. Never did Christians and Muslims have such cordial relations, collaborating in the process of trading captive individuals to transform the local economies in Africa (i.e., agriculture and ranches), in the production of civil wars to generate more captives, and in expanding the human market: bodies to work the plantations in the Americas.

The Catholic Church condoned this lucrative commerce, under the pretext of acquiring new souls. The papal bulls[7] of Nicholas V, issued in 1452, authorized the Portuguese to reduce Africans to the condition of captive individuals with the intention to Christianize them. A regulation of slavery was legislated in the Manuelinas Orders; the adoption of slavery also came to replace a great loss of labor throughout Europe because of widespread plague. The oldest register of captives sent from Africa to Brazil dates from 1533, when Pero de Góis, chief captain of the Brazilian coast, solicited the Portuguese king for the shipment of seventeen Africans to the captaincy of São Tomé (now the South Paraiba and Macaé districts in the state of Rio de Janeiro).

The Africans received the "primacy of souls," given by the Catholic Church at the beginning of 1741, when the papal bull (Bulla Immensa Pastorum) of Pope Benedict XIV, asserted that the Africans, despite their lack of faith, could be converted in the same way as all other races. We ought to clarify, however, that the soul of the Africans, as it was conceived here, signified an imposition of Christianity and its conception of the soul. Never did the Church suspect that African captives had their own concepts of a soul within their own faith; nor did it consider the profoundness of their myths and the complexity of their rituals.

The manifestation of indigenous African beliefs—of the groups concentrated principally in Bahia, Pernambuco, Maranhão, and Rio de Janeiro—brought new forms of thought and attitude in relation to the world and the universe. Among the diverse cultural groups, the Yorùbá, Angolans, and Jeje stood out for their spiritual philosophy and for a religious creed that focused on the importance of harmony with the forces living within nature, wherein we can feel and live with the divine presence of the Orixás, of the Minkisi, and the Voduns.

How was it possible for these religious traditions and cultures to survive in the Americas and in the Caribbean? Giséle Cossard called attention to the fact that "in Africa, the individuals who destabilize themselves and leave their distant forest to try for success in the city, will rapidly detach themselves from their past, abandoning their traditional faith and adorn new costumes." In this sense, everything Islamic as well as Christian "represent[ed] therefore a progress, a social promotion that favor[ed] contact, every day more numerous, with [Eurasian] civilization." She adds that this phenomenon was quite different in Brazil because the captives held onto to "their memories and owned the forces to support... this fidelity to their origins."[8]

Unlike the role played by the traditional church, African religions in the Americas acted from the beginning as true community centers that provided for the psycho-emotional care of its adherents; through millennia of botanical medicine, it looked after their health. Equally remarkable are the inheritances that it bestowed to new generations of artisans and artists of an inseparable binomial art-religion.

# A BRIEF HISTORY OF CANDOMBLÉ IN BRAZIL

The religion of the Orixá, Vodun, and Nkisi—African divinities brought by captive individuals—existed in Brazil through the influence created by the *batuque* (spiritual practice associated with drumming and dancing). In their myths, and in their rituals in the interior of the *senzulas* (slave plantation quarters), the *batuque* spoke to the captive individuals, away from the ears of the slaveholders and under the weight of official prohibition. Soon after the practice of their *batuque*, the African religions began to show their faces. However, the historical records show only the relation the faithful had with the religion of their Portuguese colonizers.

The Africans encountered in Brazil a tropical, humid climate and extensive forests, in many ways similar to what they had left in their own land. This fact became quite comprehensible in that the African religions, with their strong ligation with nature and its elements, met in Brazil the same vibrations present in their indigenous environment. The necessity to find one's *axé* (vital energy) in nature became for them, in Brazil, more crucial than in Africa, since the Portuguese oppressors deprived them of their own freedom as well as their family's privacy.

The church, whose principle incentive was the importation of captive individuals in order to protect the indigenous people (for whom they showed a little more mercy than the Africans), included the Africans in their religious ceremonies, baptizing them and making them venerate the images of Christian saints. The permission to practice the *batuque*, secured by the benevolence of the Church in relation to syncretism, normalized, in a certain sense, a clandestine practice in the forests and near the rivers. In another way, the indiscriminate oppression of all of the African cultures and their respective religions provided a great fusion of elements in the constitution of Candomblé, with the Yorùbá cosmogony as the most dominant.

Nostalgia and rebellion were feelings present at the start of the nineteenth century in Bahia. There were numerous slave revolts, as well as tentative organization in isolated *quilombos* (African hinterland settlements founded by runaway captive individuals). In a situation of common misfortune, the fight for freedom and mutual desire to recover lost Africa gave strong reasons to unite cultural enemies and traditional rivals. Conscious of this potential, the slaveholders changed their strategy in relation to the captive individuals, permitting that they regroup themselves, by "ethnicity" or "nation" on Sundays, to dance and sing in their *batuques*. An eyewitness account demonstrates the reasoning behind this approach:

> The government came to view the Batuques as an action which gratifies the Africans, insensitive and mechanically, every eight days, renewing ideas of mutual dislike which are born naturally in them, which nevertheless were fading little by little by the common disgrace; ideas which they are able to consider with the most powerful guarantee of security within the great cities of Brazil, given that if the different nations of Africa were able to forget the anger which nature had given them...the great and inevitable dangers that

> they encountered in Brazil. And who is there to
> doubt that Doom has the power of fraternizing the
> bastards? Nevertheless, since to prohibit the only
> action of disunion between the Africans comes
> to be the same that promotes the government
> indirectly to unite between themselves, how can
> they not see there will be terrible consequences.[9]

Such conduct, however, rather than provoking contradictions between the cultures, promoted a true sense of brotherhood. Once more, the permission to practice the *batuque* created the possibility of a reconstitution on Brazilian soil of the ancestral songs and dances, which facilitated (even in disguise) the veneration of African divinities.

What was crucially important was how it became possible to gather, at a single event, diverse cultures, in peaceful and apparently non-liturgical celebration. In this sense, the *batuque* served as a catalyst, combining the elements of various cultures and nations, and an example of what was to happen a few decades later in the creation of the first Candomblé meetings in Salvador.

In big cities, the Church created brotherhoods and fraternities of blacks, exclusively to look after their "souls" away from the white slaveholders. Many brotherhoods became famous because of the great number of followers. Around their protection, many African rituals were celebrated, tending to the dogmas of Christ in their façade. Protected by the brotherhood, many African religious practices were perpetuated, camouflaged as Catholic rituals. Therefore, in such cases, the idea to use the image of a Christian saint as a reference to an African divinity had nothing to do with the true adoration, given that the image was used purely as a disguise.

In many cases, the word *calundu* can be applied to specific religious activities with therapeutic purposes and oracular functions, developing not only for one person but also for a "society," or as defined by João José Reis, "a religious community in formation." Luis Nicolau Parés called attention to this phenomenon as well:

> Nevertheless, *calundu* could, in some cases, refer to organized groups with collective ritual practices that involved more participants than merely the healer-diviner and his o her clients. In 1738, the Benedictine prior of Bahia remarked that the slaves 'gather together in *societies* to perform their *calundus*.' This allusion to 'societies' is significant. In relation to the black festivities that emerged around the Recife brotherhoods, the Count of Povolide [in a 1780 letter] differentiated between 'dances that although... not the most saintly, I don't consider worthy of total censure...' and those 'superstitious dances' or 'dances that I wholly condemn.' The latter 'are those that the blacks from the Mina Coast do in secret, or in homes or in the field, having a Master Negress with an altar of idols worshipping live goats and others made of clay, anointing their bodies with various oils, rooster blood, eating corn cakes after many superstitious blessings, making the rustics believe that those rustic bread

anointings [sic] give good fortune, and make women fall in love with men and men with women.'[10]

In this way it is possible to see how the *calundus* centered less on the figure of a healer-diviner of Congo-Angola origin, but rather on the transformation of Mina Coast traditions into organized social and ritual forms, such as the *calundus* (in houses and on plantations), since during the eighteenth century, "the Jeje were demographically predominant."[11]

The word *Candomblé* was substituted for the word *calundu* in the beginning of the eighteenth century. The investigations made by historian João José Reis are extremely important since they reveal for the first time the religion of "vodun divinities" in 1830, in the region of Accú (or Acupé) in Bahia. Research carried out by Reis and Pares, using political registers and newspapers, showed a change in the leadership among African Brazilians at the start of the second half of the nineteenth century, as well as growth in the presence of mixed race and white people. Only at the start of the 1940s do we observe the preponderance of female leaders in Candomblé, to which North American anthropologist Ruth Landes in her celebrated book, *City of Women*, draws attention.

There exists an oral tradition about the origin of the first Candomblé, which claims it was barely Yorùbá in orientation. Old, freed captive individuals originally from Ketu, a city on the frontier between the Yorùbá kingdom of Oyo and Jeje kingdom of Dahomey, established the Candomblé house. The Candomblé house initially called Iyá Omi Asé Airá Intilé in Salvador, Bahia, was later re-baptized under the name Ilê Axé Iyá Nassô Oká (also known as Terreiro da Casa Branca) after its transportation to Engenho Velho, where it stands to this day. This house was the mother of other important Candomblé houses founded in the middle of the nineteenth century, such as Ilê Omin Axé Iyá Massê and Ilê Axé Opô Afonjá. The first documentary evidence, however, date only to the beginning of the year 1858, confirming the hypothesis of Parés that Candomblé had a Jeje foundation—a phenomenon previously circulated, discussed and led by Africans at the beginning of the nineteenth century. Parés also refutes, in a persuasive manner, the thesis of well-known Afro-Brazilian scholars (Verger, Bastide, Elben, and Carneiro) who believe the initial Candomblé houses arose from various African divinities and diverse cultures. Secondly, Parés did not treat this as a Brazilian innovation, since "one of the characteristics of the vodun religion is the conception of the spirit world in *constellations* or *groups* of [divinities], and one of its structural elements is the organization of congregations dedicated to the collective [religious practice] of a variable number of voduns, with public rituals that use forms of serial performance."[12] The people Parés speaks of have a long history of migrations, and of transplanting their sacred temples and their religious community spaces many years before arriving in the American colonies.

The Candomblé houses rapidly multiplied in Salvador after the emancipation of captive individuals. Their situation, however, was far from the ideals of the recently proclaimed republic—they were still marginalized, with little possibility of social ascension or honor. In Candomblé, they forged a new racial identity and new spaces to practice ancestral African religions. Given that the religious activities of African origin were not allowed in Brazil, Candomblé houses placed at the entrance of their yards altars with images of Catholic saints, giving the façade that they too were engaged in Catholic worship. Once, having been assured by the Brazilian authorities the freedom to practice African-Brazilian religions, the expediency of using the images of Catholic saints as a disguise was no longer necessary. Thus, some priestesses, led by Mãe Stella Oxossi of Ilê Axé Opô Afonjá in Salvador, initiated a campaign of "Africanization" of the yards, banishing the images of Catholic saints. However, there remains to this day yards with Catholic images that have now become a part of the tradition of that Candomblé house, dating back to more than a century of existence. The "Africanization" of the houses became part of the process of legitimizing an Afro-Brazilian identity. In Salvador during 1937, Donald Pierson calculated between seventy and one hundred Candomblé houses. Some of these were using the Nagô traditions in the orthodox form, while others declared themselves Jeje-Nagô, Jeje-Mahi, or even included many members of Bantu origin—incorporating traditions from Angola-Congo religious practices—and thus, naturally, creating a Congo or Angola Candomblé.

There were also *terreiros* which incorporated elements of indigenous shamanism, and which in turn created what is known as "Candomblés of Caboclo."[13] These are very popular in the northern regions, the interior of northeast Brazil, as well as in the state of Bahia. It is also interesting to note how the force and capability of Candomblé has spread, decisively influencing more recent religions such as Umbanda and even Tambor de Mina and Encantaria in Maranhão, and other northern states of Brazil.

# THE CANDOMBLÉ OF OUR EVERYDAY LIFE

*Whoever wants vatapá must first make the maize flour, next the palm oil, peanut, shrimp, flaked coconut, salt, adding ginger and chili at the time of seasoning... [under the specialized supervision of a] black Baiana who knows how to stir.*[14]

—Dorival Caymmi's "Vatapá" song

The black *Baiana* (woman from Bahia) is the popular image of *iaô* (children of the Orixás) in Candomblé. The *vatapá* (popular food of north and northeast Brazil, especially in Bahia), *aracajé* (Bahian dish made from peeled black-eyed peas rolled into a ball and then deep-fried), and *caruru* (Bahian shrimp component to *aracajé*) are typical delicacies of Brazilian cuisine which, especially in Bahia, are looked upon as the preferred dishes of the African divinities. Mortals enjoy these dishes also. The Brazilian actress and singer Carmen Miranda, whose renowned trademark were skirts with lace and frills, a turban full of fruit, golden rings, threads of beads and other baubles, reminds us of the *Baiana/iâo*. Her characteristic gestures when dancing—quick hand movements maneuvering in small circles around the face—are equally an allusion used in the dance of some Orixás. Another example of a popular Brazilian artist connected with the culture of Candomblé is Clara Nunes, "Warrior Clara," assumed to be the daughter of Iansã (Oya). In accordance with this association, she used white clothing similar in appearance to the outfits of *iaôs* in many music videos, and filled her repertoire of songs with references to Candomblé divinities.

Brazilian popular music is one of the areas most open to the influences of Candomblé, particularly in how it observes the explicit presence of the Orixá tradition, with many popular compositions referencing the names of various spiritual entities. Dorival Caymmi, who liked to refer to the ocean in his music, included Janaína/Iemanjá (Yemanjá) in numerous tracks of his recordings. Orisainlá (Obàtálá), Xangô (Shango), Oxóssi (Oshosi) and Oxum (Oshun) are Orixás frequently mentioned in the words of composers such as Caetano Veloso and Gilberto Gil. *Iansã, Cadê Ogum* is the title of an unforgettable piece of *samba* that helped distinguish Clara Nunes as one of the great performers of Popular Brazilian Music (MPB).

A polyrhythmic feature of MPB also expresses the strength of Orixás in the cultural life of the Brazilian people, and in popular Brazilian celebrations, many rhythms are used to evoke entities from Afro-religious traditions. This "divine presence" in the everyday life festivities of common people occurs in various forms—at times spontaneously, as in the principal *samba* schools of Rio de Janeiro, which were of course born with the protection of religious leaders and communities of black and mixed-race communities, in the *favelas* and suburbs of the city. Other times, the mode is intentional and political, such as in the organization and parades of Grêmio Recreative (Recreative Guild of Black Art) and Quilombo Samba of Palmares in Rio, or in the performances of the group Olodum in Salvador.

The carnival can be viewed as the most famous Brazilian celebration, wherein the affinity between the people and Candomblé is expressed with the most freedom. This can be seen in the traditional *Ala das Baianas* (samba school based in Rio de Janeiro), or in the renowned Afoxé Filhos de Gandhi (composed entirely by male Candomblé believers inspired by Gandhi's principles of nonviolence and peace), in the carnival of Salvador. In the Catholic ceremonies, there are Bahian street vendors celebrating their presence every year: the June feast of merrymaking known as *Penha* in Rio, or in the washing of the steps and square in front of Igreja de Nosso Senhor do Bonfim, the most famous Catholic Church in Salvador. To mark the passing of one year, the Carioca coastline is filled with people dressed in white clothing (one of the colors of Iemanjá/Yemanjá). It is possible to see various religious groups in different circles honoring their divinities, beating out rhythms with palms and singing ritualistic songs. Afterwards, they offer flowers to the powerful queen of salt waters, asking for the forthcoming year to be more prosperous than the one just passed. This ritual has been removed from Copacabana for tourist reasons, but the ceremony for Iemanjá/Yemanjá still has a strong following in Salvador, occurring traditionally on February 2.

Popular Brazilian folk stories also refer to the Candomblé religion, such as the figure Saci or Saci-pererê. Despite the popularity of this black, one-legged little boy in children's folk stories, few people are aware that his roots are the Candomblé religion as the figure Aroni, a companion of the Orixá Ossâim (Òsanyìn), father of all of the wild leaves. The writer Natália Bolívar Aróstegui once wrote that in Cuba, Aroni is considered an Exu (Eshu). Maybe because of the Exu association, the African people in Brazil spread the Saci image as a "devilish" black boy who lives to mock, and always asks people to make him a cigarette offering before entering the forest. Like the story of Saci, many other folk stories have a strong relation with the vast mythology of Candomblé, which is strengthened by the imagination of the Brazilian people when combined with the Amerindian myths; after all, both traditions (African and Amerindian) were born in tropical environments.

In everyday language, many colloquial expressions originate from the *povo do santo* (Candomblé believers). Expressions such as *ficar odara* (to be cool) and *cabeça-feita* (to get high) left the *terreiro* and gained new popularity and, sometimes, new connotations among non-believers. For example, *cabeça-feita* in Candomblé is an expression used for a person when initiated into the Candomblé religion has their head shaved, but in the popular sense can signify how drugs can enable someone to reach high spirits. *Odara* is a Yorùbá term which signifies "it's good, it's beautiful," and is widespread thanks to the songs and harmonies by Caetano Velhoso and Gilberto Gil.

The use of the *panos-da-costa* traditional shawl of the Mina coast, with its characteristic patterns, it is another mark of Candomblé that influenced Brazilian habits; in the same way, to wear white clothing on Fridays is a gesture that references the Orixá Obàtálá (Orisainlá). The popular artisans of numerous regions of Brazil are enriched by the symbolism of the Orixás as well. One notable illustration of this cultural universe is the art of Héctor Julio Páride Bernabó or Carybé. We can find drawings and engravings by him in the extensive literary work of Pierre Verger and Jorge Amado, who helped to spread Candomblé and the mysteries of the Orixás throughout the world.

Since its founding in the eighteenth century, Candomblé has been a fermentation center for the cultures brought from the gulf of Benin, including the present-day countries of Togo, Ghana, Benin, Nigeria, among others. This diversity of traditions already in dialogue in Africa, also began to bond with the

Indigenous and Portuguese cultures, generating multicultural expressions ranging from cuisine, women's fashion, forms of dance, music and drumming, idioms and even lending new vocabulary to the Portuguese language. Generated in Salvador and the Recôncavo (Brazil's largest bay), this diasporic culture, arriving in Rio de Janeiro at the second part of the nineteenth century, had influenced the fashion and behavior of the black populations. They melted this culture with their particular ways of celebration that would influence the parades and in the early twentieth century foster the emergence of the first *samba* school in the late 1920s.

# PART II

# THE RELIGION OF THE ORIXÁS

## THE AXÉ: COLORS AND FORMS

Àṣẹ (or Axé) has become a recognized term in Brazil, symbolizing in popular language "good energy" or a "tall state of mind." Its meaning is the same in the traditions of the Yorùbá, although the religious connotation has now vanished in popular use. In accordance with the traditional Yorùbá religion, àṣẹ is understood as vital energy, the true presence of the Creator (Olódúmaré) in the forces and forms of nature as well as in the minds of human beings. Axé is also, in the philosophy of Candomblé, the ability to make things happen, such as commanding spirits, the ability to invoke, to pray, and to give thanks; it is the true light of the Creator made accessible to men and women. In the Yorùbá religion, Olòrún, the supreme divinity and vital force, is the quintessential of Axé. In *Iwa-pelé: Ifá Quest,* Awo Falokun Fatunmbi gives us an idea of the appearance of Axé in this world:

> According to Ifá, the moment of Creation (Oro)
> generated a single force known as àṣẹ [axé in
> Brazil]. This force is manifest in the polar form as
> expansion and contraction. The force of expansion
> creates light, and the force of contraction
> creates matter. It is the harmonious interaction
> between light and matter that is responsible
> for good fortune, known in Yorùbá as *ire*.[15]

White, black, and red are the colors of Axé. The three colors are in tune with the chromatic manifestations of divinity in the three kingdoms: plant, mineral, and animal. The white reveals the colors of milk, semen, and secretions of the body. It represents the solar light responsible for the oxygen that we breathe throughout our life on earth. White also symbolizes the origin of all matter, uniting all colors in itself. The color white reveals the Orixá Obàtálá (Oxalá), one of the creators of the world; it is also the color of the plasma of snails, the favorite food of the Orixás. The *efun* (chalk) is white, and in Africa the landscape is made up of white clay, which when mixed with white salt can be used in many rituals. In the mineral kingdom, there are many associations with white: plate, lead, and tin. In contrast, black is associated with coal and iron, and therefore is a color of the earth. As a concrete material in the receptive form, it symbolizes the feminine principle, the uterus of nature wherein life dies, ferments, and is reborn. All of the dark colors are associated with black, including green and blue. The ashes of sacrificed animals are parts of Axé, as further examples of the black color element. Yellow and orange are related to the color red. Red is the color of the blood of humans and animals, and has an equivalent in the plant kingdom—the *azeite de dendê* (palm oil) is seen as the true divine sap. The Yorùbá consider red the supreme presence of color, because it distinguishes the potential of everything that exists now and all things that will come in the future. Copper, brass, and gold are also grouped within this color because of their warm hues.

Beyond the natural colors and elements with stones and trees, Axé is catalyzed in works of art, especially in sculptures. The Yorùbá people left behind rare objects demonstrating their wealth, and the symbolism of the elements that compose Axé. These objects transcend their ordinary functions and are transformed into pure receptacles of Axé energy.

The creation of a house of Candomblé implies the settling down of Axé. This long task involves a complex series of steps and rituals that include the preparation of sacred stones, the planting of sacred trees, and the building of the shrine to keep the Axé of each Orixá. In the contemporary world, we could say that Candomblé creates a nuclear plant for the catalyzing of Axé.

There are several body manifestations of Axé, in accordance with Yorùbá tradition. When the Creator came to the world, it materialized itself into various forms such as the boa, viper, Gabon, and even the worm. Among the birds, the divine presence is noted especially in those with a long beak, and in Africa the most popular of these is the woodpecker. Then, the Creator offered to them the ability to give and take life—Axé, the ability to make things happen. These messengers reflect the true complexity of Axé as energy. Some are dangerous, with fangs and poison, others are slow and inoffensive, but all are powerful; even the worm that has the power to ventilate and refresh the earth. Everything is part of the natural circle of life, and Axé if manifested in everything from the form of the zigzag in a lightening bolt striking down to the winding trickle of water that is born out of the mountains.

## YORÙBÁ COSMOGONY

Let us now consider the cosmogony of Candomblé from the perspective of the Yorùbá, recognizing that by leaving what we consider one pantheon of Orixás, we are now speaking about a religion that was formed in Brazil by the Jeje. The Jeje peoples imprinted their organizational and liturgical forms around a diverse range of divinities venerated, such as the Vodun, in the same way as they had done in their African lands in the Gulf of Benin. The shift from the term "Vodun" to "Orixá" signaled how the Yorùbá (principally known as Nagô in Brazil) took over the leadership of the Candomblé temples/houses in Bahia and began exporting the religion to other areas. This shift was almost seamless, since both the Jeje and Yorùbá employ the same sense of mythological deity, and of divine ancestry that corresponds to forces of nature from the sky, the water, and the forests.

Traditionally it was perceived that Voduns originating from the African continent were principally organized around divinities of fire and water, but in Brazil, they began to gain notoriety as forest divinities. Around one Vodun leader, constellations of other Voduns became engaged, like the migrating trails of the people, fleeing in the wars or in search of new conquests. In this way, new families of Voduns were constituted as with ancient satellites.

Traditional Brazilian cultural scholars believed that originally in Africa, the Orixás were venerated in a form almost monotheistic in their respective religions, and as such constituted families in Brazil. In today's social context, however, there are new theories which challenge this notion, such as the thesis of Verger and Bastide, which focuses on how the influence of the Jeje contributed to the formation of Candomblé, with its divine families, and simultaneous religious practices, in the same way in which it was already composed in African lands.

The assimilation of these hybrid forms of the Jeje-Yorùbá for Candomblé is extremely easy given the fact that there is a similarity between the Voduns and Orixás. Their attributions and qualities seem to derive from the same cosmological vision of the world. As human beings, both inside and outside ourselves, we have an equilibrium governed by our relation with an ethical commitment, in harmony with the forces of nature. The Orixás and Voduns are forces that are in nature and once embodied by humans, strengthen and drive us to a more fulfilled life. The Jeje-Yorùbá pantheon reflects a multicultural and plural vision of human behavior; every Orixá or Vodun governing a region of nature in the diversity of the animal, plant, and mineral kingdoms evokes attitudes, reflections, contemplations, and possible resolutions of problems. In the culture of the Vodun-Orixá, the individual not only prostrates before a force of nature greater than him- or herself, but searches within to find a force that lies dormant—or in latter times—that has been massacred or even forgotten by a society focused on the immediate consumption and contempt of nature. The reestablishment of these forces, outside and inside our heads, and in the sacred parts of the body, reflects the true sense of religion.

Often, the Orixás venerated in Brazil present elements of Jeje origin, but through the analysis of the original Yorùbá symbolism, it is sometimes surprising that certain elements appear to be rooted in one religion when in fact they originate in another.

For example, the Nagô in the Candomblé of Brazil generally use the word *vodun* to signify the most sacred forces in existence. The true settlement of Exu often has its roots not in Yorùbá, but rather in Jeje origins.

Originally, the Supreme Being of the Yorùbá was represented by the trilogy Olofi-Olódúmaré-Olòrún. From this perspective, the divine is something absolute that hovers above everything and everybody, an intrinsic part of the Yorùbá metaphysics. Although certain aspects of this trinity are similar to the Christian Holy Trinity, it must not be compared or even perceived as the result of syncretism; Yorùbá cosmogony existed many centuries before the arrival of the first Catholic priests in Africa. In accordance with the Yorùbá cosmogony, the Supreme Being projects itself into three entities: Olofi, the Creator and direct contact with the Orixás and humans; Olódúmaré, the universal law in itself, symbolizing the subjection to the law of nature; and Olòrún, the sun and the vital force that represents all energy in the earth and sky.

In many myths, Olofi is considered the creator of the world. Olofi was so powerful that it made this task look easy; although it is one thing to make something, it is quite another to get it working. When Olofi distributed the jobs among his sons he explained to them that humans are always fighting amongst themselves, and so he was compelled to make Ayguna, the Orixá of inclinations. Because Olofi is a complete being and always at peace, he could not comprehend why Ayguna was always stirring up fights. One day he pleaded with his son to stop. However, Ayguna responded, "If we do not have discord we do not have progression, because when two people wish for something, then four people will wish it." Olofi said fine, but "if it is so, the world will continue until the day that you give them the sword of war and you lay down to rest." This day has still not arrived, but Olofi chose to delude himself, and decided to no longer intervene in human destiny.

Olofi was born from nothing, by himself, living a secluded life and coming few times to the world. Olofi is particularly not remembered in Brazil. His representation as an old man with a white head of hair, tired, and dressed in white clothing can be confused with Oshalá (Obàtálá), father of all the other Orixás.

Olodumare is the manifestation of everything that exists, the universe and all its components. For him, nothing can be lost and it is not possible to contact him. He is an indecipherable being and the pronunciation of his name should be followed by a reverence, such as touching the ground with your fingers. The myth of the creation of Ifá teaches us that all the forms were set into the universe at the beginning of time. The primal spirit that supported the form as an element of creation is Olodumare. Some Yorùbá-English dictionaries define Olodumare as "God in himself." In the metaphysical meaning, this signifies that Olodumare is an aspect of Olorun that has physical existence. In this form, Olodumare can be compared with the Western theological concept known as pantheism—the belief that everything in the physical universe is an expression of divinity. Olodumare could be understood as an archetype or repository of all forms that are given configuration in matter; a universal symbol of substance.

Olorun, in the popular understanding, is the sky, but he can also have a more profound meaning when interpreted as vital energy. We can feel his presence, but we are not able to touch it; he is visible only through the rays of the sun. He is a source of energy and light. It is common for the *babalawo* (*babalaô* in Brazil) to greet Olorun by raising their hands, with the palms facing upwards, towards the sun.

According to the Nagô tradition in Brazil, the being who ordered Oshalá (Obàtálá) to create the world was Olorun and not Olofi, as is believed in Cuba. Oshalá called all of the other Orixás to go with him to create the world. Odùduwà was the only one that could not go, because she had a duty to give an offering to Olorun. Therefore, all of the other Orixás followed Obàtálá and Odùduwà remained. On the way, Obàtálá met Exu, who reminded him that he too had to fulfill certain duties before he traveled. However, Obàtálá did not heed the advice and continued on his journey. Along the way, he began feeling thirsty after traveling some distance; he viewed a palm tree and, without being able to control himself, he opened a hole in the side of the palm with his Opaxoró cane and greedily drank the palm wine until he passed out.

Meanwhile, Odùduwà went to consult the Ifá divination system before making her offering in accordance to what was revealed by the *babalaô*. The last thing that she had to do was to take an offering to Olorun. He became angry, however, when he noticed that she did not follow the others as he had ordered. She argued that she was only obeying the orders from Ifá, and so Olorun accepted the offering with gratitude. At that moment, Olorun remembered there was something more important for the creation of the world he had forgotten to deliver to Obàtálá: a sack of earth. Odùduwà was therefore put in charge of taking the sack to Obàtálá, and so with the sack on her back, she traveled in search of him. When she finally met up with him, Obàtálá was in an unconscious state with the other Orixás around him. Odùduwà tried to revive him but with no success; therefore she took the sack of earth, placed it once more on her back, and returned to the feet of Olorun. He decided to give to Odùduwà the task of creating the world and so she carried the sack to the place chosen by Olorun, and created it herself.

The myth of creation reminds us of the risks of not fulfilling the Ifá prescriptions. For religious followers, the first consultation with Ifá is popularly known as the *jogo do búzios* (the game of *búzios* or cowrie shells divination), and is a religious practice that must always take place before an offering. *Dar um obrigação* (to give a duty) is the same as a votive offering. In the myth of the creation of the word, Esu is the guardian of the divination systems, and later we will see that he is also the messenger between the Orixás and humans.

The Nagô mythology is present in Candomblé even outside the houses where the Orixás are venerated, although their secrets are kept only by the initiated. The Orixás mythologies also became part of Umbanda (another important Afro-Brazilian religion that has influences from Bantu Africa), Alan Kardec's Spiritualism, Indigenous and Catholic traditions but where the Orixás govern all other entities, due to their status as archetypes and deified ancestors. In addition, even those people who have no relationship with Candomblé or Umbanda, when they have problems that cannot be solved in their Catholic, Protestant, or Evangelical churches know that the doors of the Candomblé houses are open. Candomblé practitioners know how to solve problems of justice with Xangô/Shango, Oshun for love, health with Omulu or Yemanjá, and money problems with Exu. There is a corpus of oral knowledge recounting the Nagô tradition; this same tradition is brought to bear on the carnivals in Rio, Salvador, and other large cities and in the *samba* schools that reenact this rich mythology.

## THE ORIXÁS AND NATURE

Throughout this book, I frequently mention the intimate connection between the Orixás and nature, specifically emphasizing the importance of plants and natural environments for the Candomblé liturgy.

To apprehend of the concept of "Axé," notions and experiences that are seen to elevate the faithful to states of mystic comprehension of nature, promoting the communion between the visible and invisible beings that inhabit it, frequently permeate the path of an apprentice to the Orixá religion. This is why Candomblé strongly supports the use of divination systems as a form of direct communication with the intelligent forces of nature (Orixás) and with the other spirits, which are expressed through natural phenomena.

After the world was created, every Orixá received a part of Axé, which gave them the power over the diverse types of beings and things, which were manifested in the material world. Every Orixá represents a different force in nature, and through refining our sensitivity, we can ascertain that the presence of an Orixá is alive in the natural environments to which they correspond. Therefore, Oshun (spring water) can be found within the rivers and waterfalls; Oxalá (air) and Oya/Iansã (wind) are accessible in the altitude of the mountains; Iemanjá/Yemanjá on the beaches; and Oxóssi (hunter), Ossâim (leaves), and Ogum/Ogun (iron, masculine earth forms) are localized in the forests. If you want to commune with Xangô/Shango (thunder), though, it is best to remain close to a good piece of stone since it could be very risky to be near a lightning conductor during a storm. These principles demonstrate the ways that certain natural environments can function through divination systems, wherein the interaction with the elements can support self-awareness and the resolution of human problems.

The writer Awo Falokun Fatunbi, a priest of Ifá, suggests to beginners the above principle wherein an Orixá is one of the fundamental elements (earth, fire, water, or air) for use in study and prayer. The elements, when analyzed metaphysically, can be applied to specific questions of the human soul and shed light on our pitfalls and our pathway to spirituality. The intersection of these two points can be approached in relation to the explicit connection between the divine, the human, and the natural universe.

Orixás associated with the air (Oxalá/Odùduwà) are generally associated with ethical issues and positive nature and are often invoked when considering metaphysical questions or the nature of creation. Orixás associated with the earth (Ogum/Oxóssi/Ossâim) emphasize questions of survival, such as ecology, healthcare, and home security. They also guide artistic tasks such as sculpture and metalwork. Orixás associated with water (Iemanjá/Olokum) are nurturers; they are related to mental health and physics. The element of water (Oshun) is also essential for questions of fertility and abundance, which in the Yorùbá culture signify a rich and joyful life. Orixás associated with fire (Xangô/Agayú) are found within the core of all processes of transformation. Passion is considered an aspect of fire, and includes personal relationships as well as social justice issues. Fire is also an element that tempers the head during the inaction process in Candomblé.

In the Candomblé of the Yorùbá, Iroko is a tree of great importance, as it symbolizes the Tree Orixá. Tying a white sash around the trunk honors this Orixá; other plants are also dignified in this way, but using sashes in different colors. In the general sense, the importance of trees in Candomblé can be seen in the well-known phrase, "Every time that Oshalá (Obàtálá) created a person, they also create a tree."

The concepts developed by some priests in relation to the purposes and lessons of nature are the consequence of a life dedicated to the Orixás and the practices of Candomblé. Of course not everyone can or wants to submit to the severe rules of initiation in the Candomblé *terreiros*; it is a long process, culminating in a priesthood that requires exclusive dedication to the divinities and a lifelong commitment to their ideals. Alternatively, many people construct a small altar in the home, upon which they place objects and elements that symbolize the energy that connects the Orixás and nature. For instance, for the Orixás of air, a white towel, saucer, or candle is used. Likewise, some use organic chalk and white shells, especially the ones with a spiral design; or white stones, eggs, white fabric, or jewels of white precious stones. A little blue light is used to symbolize the sky. Photos and drawings of the sun, with the manifestation of light, are placed together on the altar, along with mandalas representing the unification of nature.

For the Orixás of salt water, a little seawater and stones removed from a beach are used—or even a bit of salt in tap water. For Orixás of sweet water, the colors green and yellow and the stones of a river or lake are used instead. Meditation with a mirror is considered an exercise of self-knowledge. For Orixás of fire, red candles surrounded by volcanic rocks are appropriate; and the double-edged axe symbolizes Xangô, decorated in red and white. Between the Orixás of the earth, the altar of Oxóssi is the most simple, made with "dirt" stones taken from a favorite place in nature and placed about the altar with a bow and arrow.

In Africa, the altars are centers of attraction for specific forces of nature. The Orixás are attracted to them after successive repetitions of prayers, songs, and invocations. The orations are meant to be performed with discipline, throughout the year, and only when help is truly necessary. In this way the presence of the Orixá of the altar is strongest.

The first orations of a beginner should be very simple: a person commences by saying their name, and then asks that a certain Orixá listen to their prayer, thanking them for the family from which they came. Once this is complete, the request can be made. Every time that such a request is placed, an offering accompanies it; this offering makes up an especially complex and detailed part of the religion. However, the component most valued in any offering is the disposition in the supplicant's hands; they are urged to remember, according to the Candomblé traditional thoughts, "the sincerity of the gesture which is important." By making an offering, supplicants are using the ritual to say that they do not expect to receive something for nothing. A true offering is a commitment to live a life in harmony with nature and to appreciate its many blessings.

# THE ORIXÁS AND THEIR ARCHETYPES

Renowned psychiatrist Carl G. Jung did not include specific studies of African myths in his vast oeuvre, but he can still be used as a useful source when considering a contemporary approach to the concepts of the Yorùbá mythology—specifically, how their archetypical figures are incorporated in rituals and venerated by millions of people in Africa and the Americas. By applying some of these concepts, we can understand more easily how the meaning of every Orixá permeates the daily life of Candomblé congregations. According to Jung, archetypes are psychological images revealing the information contained in the collective unconscious, which, in turn, store experiences and knowledge that have belonged to all humankind since the dawn of time.

An archetype is not a defined signal, though subject to immediate understanding; it is, firstly, a symbol, which is continuously evolving through time, given that it stimulates an association in the mind of each individual. In this sense, direct contact with an archetype personality of an Orixá provides a personal and intimate experience in relation to the subjects and issues that have affinity with the Orixá.

The Orixás are archetypal personalities that explore through their myths a variety of mystic teachings about diverse areas of existence. Candomblé is the religious practice that has direct access to all these wellsprings of ancestral knowledge. We can say that there exists, basically, two types of relationships with the Orixás: the first is more passionate and emotional, and is encountered during rituals, initiation, and possession. The second is more philosophic and active, and is evolved gradually though divination system consultations, study, offerings, and prayers.

In the Candomblé *terreiros*, the initiate usually takes on the personality of their "Orixá-of-the-head" and, in many occasions, arrives through calling the name of that divinity. Researcher Monique Augras, in her thesis on religious psychology, observes that this proceeding is part of the manifestation of the double (Orixá) in the life of the *filho-do-santo* ("son of the Orixá"; male initiate). Despite awareness of the mutual dependence between the Orixá and the initiated, Augras's study frequently references the "ruler-of-the-head" as being a "strange and powerful other.... However, a metamorphosis which occurs during the rituals of integral possession is the 'I' personality of the initiate with the divine 'Other' and this union of human initiate with their transcendental double and archetype is an authentic expression of a unique mythic identity."

Through the *jogo de búzios*, the contemplation of nature and other divination system practices, a person can effectively communicate themselves with the Orixás. Every Orixá responds, alerts, or resolves problems subject to their specific area of action, corresponding with the archetype represented by the Orixá. In a similar sense, Orixás can also possess spaces within Candomblé *terreiros* and in nature. Contemplation of certain natural landscapes, sitting on the front door of an Orixá's *casa* (house) in order to think a little, or even choosing the vegetables to put down for an offering—all of these actions will allow us to reflect upon the latent meanings within the archetype of an Orixá. By doing this, we can amplify our knowledge about a special part of ourselves, of nature, and of life.

Let us now resume our description of the personality and the attributes of the Orixás most known in Brazil. Obviously, I will start with Exu, given that he is always the first to be honored and, as we shall learn, also extremely vindictive!

# EXU/ELÉGUA: ORIXÁ OF DIRECTIONS
## IN SPACE AND TIME

Exu/Eshu is a messenger, responsible for the communication between the temporal world (Ayé) and the world of the divinities (Orun). In this aspect, Exu is an analogy to the divinity Mercury, found in Greco-Roman mythology. He is the Orixá of all the paths and all the directions. For this reason, the offerings intended for him must be placed on crossroads.

Money and sex, which are fundamental components of the material exchange between people, are also of great interest to him; this side of Exu is quite explicit in the Umbanda religion. His great ability to create action in the physical world, while being indifferent to good and bad, teaches us that nature can be a blunt and bipolar force in eternal movement. This force can realize the desire for wickedness in a person, so be warned; it will not protect you should you choose to develop evil practices in life. This concept is often misunderstood when people say that Exu is "vindictive." Even though the difficult temperament of Exu creates enemies with the majority of the Orixás, there are still some studies claiming that every Orixá is accompanied by a "specialized Exu" that assists them in their work.

Exu is always dealing with two sides of everything without committing himself to a single outcome; in so doing, he provokes confusion and misunderstandings, showing people always the more reflective path rather than rushing to radical, passionate, or hurried judgments. One myth describes an occasion in which Exu painted the right half of his body red and the other half black, and then challenged two friends to place a bet, stating that whoever was able to distinguish his color would win an incredible reward. The two thought this would be easy, but each one was only able to see one-half of Exu's body. The outcome was that they disagreed so much that they ended up fighting; Exu laughed out loud and afterwards mocked them, stating, "How will you know what I am if you do not turn me around?" He also symbolizes the initial chaos that precedes creation, the organization of things in the world or in a person's life. To survive this aspect of Exu, it is said that a person's best option is to develop initiative and be aware that there are two sides of everything, and to understand this balance. In practical terms, it is recommended that before one performs a ritual, one should first honor him to avoid later problems, as he is the messenger of the Orixás.

His presence is very strong in the Candomblé of Brazil, and although it is rare to find people initiated for Exu, any Candomblé ritual cannot begin without honoring him. His colors are black and red, and his day is Monday. In the Candomblé Jeje he is called Legua or Elégua.

## OGUM/OGUN: ORIXÁ OF IRON AND WAR

The Yorùbá divinity of iron, patron of blacksmiths, farmers, hunters and all those who use this metal is known in Brazil as Ogum—the Orixá of war and the masculine polarity of the earth element. Aggression and violence are his characteristics, and according to folklore, he was able to use them to open a space in the world, conquering the resources that guaranteed his survival. He is the pioneer, using his knife to create the first prick in the virgin forest, "deflorating" it.

His expertise is in manual skills. Activities that demand techniques such as agriculture and war are under his command. He is able to use the same iron to make beautiful sculptures as to make machines, ploughs, and weapons. Currently, industry and transport can be included in this field to the extent that Ogum is considered the patron of motorists. Ogum is the Orixá who goes first—every moment he is starting new things, opening routes, and expanding humanity's frontiers.

Ogum represents virility, indomitable energy, and the capacity to generate forces for us to overcome our most difficult obstacles. This force is the survival instinct, the thirst for independence and self-determination. In Brazil, the captive Africans and their descendants emphasized his affinity with war, since Ogum inspired their escapes into the interior of the forest, revolts, and insurrections against European persecutors.

Ogum's stormy, bellicose temperament and his lack of patience can sometimes cause him great suffering. At feasts, he appears immediately after Exu, and he goes in front opening the way for the other Orixás. When he arrives at the Candomblé ground for veneration, he is greeted with the shout, "Ogum iééé!" ("Hail Ogum!"). His day is Tuesday, and his principle color is blue and sometimes green. In Cuba, he is associated with Saint John the Baptist and Saint Peter; in Bahia with Saint Anthony, and in Rio with Saint George.

## OXÓSSI: KING OF TROPICAL FORESTS

Oxóssi is both a hunter and protector of animals, and for this reason, he does not tolerate those who kill them unnecessarily. He has the skill to secure trails in the middle of the forest, to locate and fell prey without batting an eyelid. It is for this reason that the priests of Ifá recommend that supplicants offer prayers to Oxóssi when uncertain of the problem that afflicts them, or what specific part of their consciousness needs changing.

Oxóssi lives in the forest together with the animals and in great harmony with nature. However, at the same time, he is a representative of a cultural universe because he goes to find the hunt to bring it back to his people, for which he receives honor. In many Candomblé myths, Oxóssi is represented as a hero. He was born as an average person, who because of his actions during his lifetime and his unparalleled abilities, he was reborn divine.

Oxóssi represents an obstinate impulse, because he brings the awareness of a clear task to carry out, and he sees it through to the end. For hunting, he uses the *ofá* (bow) and *damatá* (arrow), which always finds its mark. His dance imitates hunting and following the tracks of animals on the ground inside the shed in the place of veneration. When he appears, he is greeted by the cry, "Oké!"

In truth, it seems that he is more interested in work above all things. His work made him choose to abandon the mother Iemanjá in order to live in the forest with Ossâim. His day is Thursday and his colors are light blue and green.

# IROKO: A TREE ORIXÁ

Iroko is a tree Orixá. Given that the Iroko tree is indigenous to Africa, in Brazil it is represented by a white *gameleira* tree, and you will find one planted in any traditional *terreiro*. One of Iroko's myths tells us how this tree never dies, even when a terrible drought demolished all plant life thanks to a fight between the sky and the earth. The immense size of the tree gives it significance—Iroko is both deeply rooted whilst at the same time touches celestial heights with its branches and leaves.

In the Cuban Candomblé houses, Iroko is a pathway for Oshalá, and the wood from its trunk is used as the staff of Olofi. According to Candomblé believers, all the Orixás come to Iroko, and it is possible to praise them by bending in front of its roots. If someone desires children, they can ask Iroko, repeating their request every year. Once the baby arrives, the parents must offer a sheep in thanks to this Orixá; if forgotten, they can provoke Iroko's implacable wrath.

In the Candomblé garden, outside the *terreiro*, Iroko occupies a prominent place. Around its trunk, a piece of white fabric is tied to give it dignity; between its largest roots, we see many offerings. In the Candomblé from the Congo-Angola line, it is called *Tempo* or *Katende*; in the Candomblé of Jeje origin, its name is Loko. In every case, it represents the spiritual capability of the tree: a link between the sky and earth, between spiritual and material life from which the harmony of life comes. For all of this, human beings as well as the Orixás equally respect Iroko. Its day is Tuesday, and white is its color.

# OSSÂIM/ÒSANYÌN: ORIXÁ OF WILD LEAVES

*Without leaves, no Orixá*

—Candomblé saying

This traditional Candomblé saying proves the importance of Ossâim, who owns all liturgical and medicinal leaves, whose sacred power is indispensable even for the divinities. He is a healer because he knows the secrets of the forest, the plants that kill, and those that cure. His teachings are secretive and mysterious, and his power in Candomblé is strong, since the use of leaves is indispensable in all the rituals. It is a green leaf, responsible for photosynthesis, which transforms solar energy into organic energy: the beginning of the vital circle of life in the earth ecosystem.

Ossâim does nothing without a price. Whoever asks something from him should first leave some coins in the entrance of a forest, as it is believed that he would demand payment from even his own mother. This notion of exchange within nature is similar to one of the fundamental ideas belonging to the indigenous Caiapós group: "If we take something from nature, we must enrich it still more." This phrase reminds us that whilst natural resources are finite, their capacity for transformation is not.

The symbol of Ossâim is even, sharp spears pointing upwards with a bird balancing on the point of the central spear. It is difficult to imagine him in a human form, since he is intimately connected to the very soul of the forest. The day of Ossâim is, for some, Monday; for others, it is Thursday or Saturday. His colors are green and yellow, or green, white, and brown.

## OMOLU-OBALUIÊ: ORIXÁ OF ILLNESSES AND CURES

Omolu-Obaluiê is an Orixá of smallpox, and of epidemics in general; he can both cause illnesses and cure them, often being considered the medicine of the poor. He is a very severe divinity who deserves respect. Some of his several names reference the fact that he is the Orixá of all of the spirits of the earth; the other names can no longer be uttered, since they can bring disgrace upon those who utter them.

Omolu-Obaluiê also represents the deep internal fire of the earth, which explodes in volcanoes and other eruptions; perhaps because of this, his human body shows open wounds. He chooses to live all covered in straw in order to hide these wounds and sores. He knows the mysteries of death and rebirth; his teachings are so dangerous that they can only be transmitted to people who are specially initiated to his mysteries.

Omolu-Obaluiê is associated with Saint Lazarus, and in Umbanda he is the leader of the group of entities from the cemetery. The punitive character of the Omolu-Obaluiê martyrdoms is similar to many of the Catholic beliefs about the necessity of confessions.

In general, we can say Omolu-Obaluiê represents the unpleasant aspects of existence that we are unable to ignore. This Orixá encourages us to be aware of the negative side of our consciousness and how to address undesirable aspects of ourselves. He reminds us that the true cause of all illnesses is in the unhealthy retention of that which must die for life to continue its cycle of renewal.

When Omolu-Obaluiê dances at the Candomblé feasts, he appears like a small pile of straw that suddenly bursts into life. He wears raffia clothing, strands of which also cover his face to hide the smallpox scars and to warn of dangerous contagion. From his own suffering Omolu-Obaluiê has achieved the power to cure the illness of others. However, he is also very stern, using smallpox to punish those who do evil and who do not respect him. He is the son of Nanã Buruku and brother of Oxumaré/Oshunmare; like them, he does not accept sacrifices that involve the use of metal knife. His day of the week is Monday, and the colors in his necklace are alternating black and white beads. In Cuba, white with royal blue and purple is used.

## OXUMARÉ/ÒSÙMÀRÈ: THE RAINBOW SNAKE

Oxumaré/Òsùmàrè is a serpent that lives winding around the world, and is believed to create the rainbow. The serpent is a symbol of creation, human procreation, and the link between the temporal world and that of the ancestors. For six months of the year, this serpent is a man, and the other six months it is a woman that goes by the name of Bessém. As an Orixá of the earth, he/she represents the hidden wealth of the underground world, performing the function of bringing water back to the palace of Xangô in the sky, thus guaranteeing the perpetuation of the water cycle for plants. Candomblé also states that Oxumaré (Oshunmare) is the divinity of sound, the arts, and beauty.

His/her principal characteristic is duality, and perhaps because of this he/she is an Orixá that is demanding and inconstant. In the form of the snake, he/she is dangerous, but in the form of the rainbow, beneficial and extremely beautiful. His/her eternal movement keeps the world from coming undone.

For the priests of Ifá, Oshunmare is the messenger of Olódúmaré. In this sense, Oshunmare represents the pact between the divinities and humans. It reminds us of the biblical passage in which, after the flood, the Christian God created a rainbow to express the promise that the world would never again be destroyed by water. The rainbow is the visible spectrum of lights that the powers of Oshunmare manifest; it is a bridge between humans and the divine—a visible phenomenon of a mysterious divinity, an image of that which is too difficult to be defined.

Oshunmare dances by revolving around his/her own body, pointing successively to the ground and to the sky. His/her necklaces are of yellow and green (or black) beads. His/her initiates also wear a *brajá*, a necklace of cowrie shells connected like scales of a serpent's skin. The day of this Orixá is Tuesday. Offerings to him/her are made with beans, corn, and shrimp cooked in palm oil.

## NANÃ BURUKU (NANA BULUKU): GREAT MOTHER OF THE MARSHES

Nanã Buruku predates the Iron Age, and for this reason, she does not accept animals sacrificed with a knife. She is the mud, and queen of the stagnant water of lakes and swamps. The fine rain that makes the ground slippery is related to Nanã. She is the mother of the dead, whom she keeps in the dark depths of the earth. She originates from the Benin Republic, the old kingdom of Dahomey and Togo, and is the mother of Omolu, Oshunmare, and, for some, Ossâim. The Yorùbá people tell the myth of how she gave birth to Orixás with deformities, one with smallpox, another with the body of a serpent, and one crippled.

Nanã is regarded as a dangerous divinity; she does not tolerate disrespectful people and never forgets offenses against her. Her power over the dead frequently presents a threat to the patriarchy. She is profoundly aware of the necessity of death, and this is the cornerstone of her principal teachings. The more grave and severe aspects of Nanã's personality represent the ability elderly women have to command authority within the nuclear family. She has a grandmother aspect, a figure who does not hesitate to distribute punishments in order to educate the young in social rules and religious precepts.

The *ibiri* that symbolizes her is made of straw from the palm tree, tied in a bundle, with a curved upper part. This represents the multitude of the deceased, and she carries it in her arms like a baby. She dances in a serious, dignified manner, supported by an imaginary staff, imitating the slow and difficult steps of the aged. Her followers wear necklaces of white beads with blue stripes, and they offer her she-goats and Guinea hens. She is honored on Monday or on Saturday, and lilac is her principal color. She is associated with Saint Ana in Brazil, and Our Lady of Carmo or Saint Teresa in Cuba. In Candomblé Angola, she is called Mameto Zumba.

# SHANGO/XANGÔ: ORIXÁ OF JUSTICE

Virile, daring, and righteous, Xangô punishes liars and thieves. Noted for his pride, he is never willing to take second place. Legends describe him as an ardent lover, who braids his hair and wears decorative bands and bracelets. He is one of the most honored Orixás in Brazil. Within nature, his form is thunder, the fire of the sky. He was the fourth king in the ancient Yorùbá city of Oyo, who was able to control the lightening bolts through magic.

His sense of righteousness and duty towards community is more powerful than his own attachment to life. In fact, the existence of Xangô is incompatible with death, given that, as a master of fire, he is a representation of a vital impulse. His vitality is so great that his followers almost never enter the cemetery. Some stories say, however, that he committed suicide, shaming himself, because his undesirable behavior provoked a great disgrace; according to the myth, he ordered two of his subjects (brothers) to complete a very difficult task that led them to fight and ended in their killing each other. Xangô does not like to remember this episode and for this reason, those faithful to him are accustomed to say for his health, "The king that did not kill himself."

The *oxé* (double-headed axe), in the stylized form of a man with twin fires on his head, symbolizes this Orixá. Xangô is a conqueror; his talent with women brought him marriages with Oshun, Oba, and Oya, his most constant companion, with whom he divided the ability of fire. Another trait of his great character is his sensuality and his appetite for sex, food, and drink.

Those who venerate Xangô wear necklaces of red and white beads and offer sheep as sacrifices. Amalá, a dish made from yam flour with okra in palm oil sauce, is Xangô's favorite. One of his names in the Angolan Candomblé is Zazi, derived from *nzazi*, the Kikongo word for lighting. Among the *voduns* from Togo and Benin, he is called Hervioso. His day of the week is Wednesday. He is associated with Saint Geronimo in Brazil, but in Cuba, curiously, he is linked with Saint Barbara.

# IANSÃ/OYA: LADY OF THE WIND AND STORMS

She is the divinity of the wind and storms. The archetype of Oya represents the more active aspect of the feminine universe. This powerful and authoritarian Orixá wages war with weapons in her hand as well as diverse magic tricks that disguise her from enemies by transforming her into animals and other such things. She can be seen as an Amazon woman, although at certain times she still needs men. Among her many companions, Xangô is the most constant.

Some stories describe her as being a good companion, with no prejudices. When she was married to Ogum, she helped him work at the anvil, and she danced with Omolu-Obaluiê, the Orixá of the smallpox, even when his body was covered with sores. (Because of this, he gave her power over the dead.)

As an active woman, she cannot always be at her children's side. Some legends tell us that she taught her children specific signs with which to call her. After this, she secured a path through the world, making things always new and fighting on the side of her preferred husband. Supplicants turn to her when wanting to make a necessary life change, in either their conscience or personality.

Oya also has power over the *Egungun* (ancestors), which hold her in high regard. Other characteristics of her personality are perceptiveness and fraternity. Oya shows us maturity in women, through her ability to look closely at the ugly things in life without fear or prejudice. She is a woman who knows many things, who is strong and aggressive, but also knows how to be jovial and seductive.

Her day is Wednesday and her principal color is red. In Cuba, she is associated with the Virgin of Candelaria, Virgin of Carmen, and Saint Teresa of Jesus; in Brazil with Saint Barbara.

# OXUM/OSHUN: QUEEN OF THE SPRING WATERS

Oshun is the divinity of spring waters: she possesses a kind seduction in the sweetness of her voice and the delicacy of her gestures. She rules over fertility and is the source of children. She represents a passive female whose body perpetuates life. We can see her force in the miracle of birth, which gives light to a new being, alive and full of health.

Oshun may be deceitful, selfish, and self-willed, but provides a life of wealth and pleasure. One legend tells us that she can win a war without fighting, because she can take so long grooming herself that her enemies are defeated whilst she gazes into the mirror. She is highly mannered and delicate, like the flow of the streams among the rocks, but also as powerful as the great waterfalls, which generate electricity but whose true force is gravity; or like the flowers, beautiful and perfumed, that attract birds and insects, which are the true agents of pollination. Oshun is effortlessly wealthy because her admirers heap gifts upon her. The graces of this divinity are like the miracle of life, and manifest everywhere in the world through the female of all species—and Oshun herself knows this all too well.

The colors of Oshun are yellow and golden; her day of the week is Saturday. In Brazil, she can be associated with Our Lady of Candelas and Our Woman of Thanks; in Cuba, with our Woman of Charity and Copper.

# IEMANJÁ/YEMANJÁ: QUEEN OF THE SEA WATERS

Her name derives from a Yorùbá expression that means "the mother whose children are fish." In Brazil, she is the most important and most popular female Orixá. Iemanjá is the mother, always dividing herself for the needs of her children. Besides her own children, she takes care of other children rejected by other divinities. In nature she is represented by the shallow seawater found near the shore; the deep waters are considered the purview of Olokun, a divinity relatively unknown in Brazil.

On New Year's Eve in Rio, it is customary for people from all religions to make offerings to Iemanjá, asking her that the forthcoming year be better than the previous one. Because of her goodness and her maternal nature, Iemanjá is associated with the Virgin Mary. In Yorùbá mythology, she was combined with Oshalá to give birth to various Orixás.

Iemanjá is so maternal that she will always turn a blind eye to ignore the deficiencies of her offspring, but she can also be possessive and resort to emotional extortion so that her "eternal children" never distance themselves from her. In this sense, she is a good representation of a Brazilian mother: obliging, overprotective, and utterly devoted to her children. She can be invoked to promote in supplicants a true spiritual cleansing, a healing from the sufferings and emotional injuries that prevent continuing evolution.

When Iemanjá dances, she places her hands alternately on her forehead and her neck, undulating like the waves of the sea. Silver armbands, crown, and fan are all typical of this Orixá. Her *axé* emanates from rocks and shells from the sea. Her day of the week is Saturday; her colors are white and blue. In Brazil, she is associated with Our Lady of the Immaculate Conception; in Cuba, with the Virgin Saint of Regla. When she appears, she is greeted with the cry, "Odó iyá!" (Mother of the river).

## OXALÁ (OSHALÁ)/OBÀTÁLÁ: THE CREATOR OF HUMAN BEINGS

He is the great father, creator of Orixás and all human beings. Oxalá (Oshalá) in Brazil, Obàtálá is the Orixá of purity who brings with him the symbolic principle of everything, since purity is represented by white, the mixture of all colors. He is also connected with the air and the celestial heights.

As the archetype of a great father, Obàtálá is unshakable in his authority and extremely generous in his wisdom. In human life, Obàtálá is related to the formulation of ideas and their manifestation in human character (and in our minds). He provokes creativity and guides ethical behavior. Given that he is the supreme authority, Obàtálá can be very stubborn; he refuses to follow the recommendations of others because he believes he should act only of his own volition. Thus, drunk on palm wine, Obàtálá lost the "bag of creation" and with it the right to make the world. Responsible for creating the bodies of human beings from clay into which life would breathe; he shapes both the able-bodied and the deformed. He has an audacious and independent temperament, never pausing to listen to the opinions of others.

Obàtálá represents masculine and creator principles. His personality incorporates two very different aspects. One of these is personified through the young Obàtálá, a warrior depicted in the restless Oshanguian in Brazil or Ayaguna in Cuba; the other is the old Obàtálá, more grandfather than father, a knowledgeable man and a good councilor, whose name is Oxalufan. He is the last Orixá to appear at Candomblé public rituals; walking with difficulty, he is supported by his magic staff and protected by the other Orixás and ritual helpers.

His day of the week is Friday; on this day Candomblé followers use white clothing to honor him. Obàtálá is also light blue, which represents the sky during the day. In Cuba, as well as in Brazil, Obàtálá is associated with Jesus Christ.

# OTHER ORIXÁS AND ENTITIES

### THE ÌBEJÌ

The Ìbejì are twins, a boy and a girl, children of Oshun and Xangô, who were created by Iemanjá. It is common to see them associated with Saint Cosme and Saint Damian. They protect children; as children themselves, they like sweets, soft drinks, and to play and have fun. They enjoy being given paternal affection from all of the Orixás. Some Cuban legends say that they are able to make life "hell" even to the Christian Devil with frenetic music that is played on their wooden drums. They represent the renovation of spirit, the birth of a new interior life.

## THE ERÉ

Olga G. Cacciotore defines "eré" as children belonging to the vibrating current of an Orixá. Every *Iyawo* or initiate has a particular *ère* that corresponds to the Orixá *dono da cabeça* (the Orixá who is "head owner" for an individual) that assists the initiated in understanding what to do in the Candomblé reclusion room called *camarinha* (small room) or *rondaime*. Each *eré* orally transmits the orders and desires of the Orixás, who talk very little and only with the initiated.

The *eré* perform the function of an intermediate force between humans and the Orixás during rituals. In this sense, the action of the *eré* is an analogue that is realized for Exu in the divination system of Ifá and the tradition of the Orixás, since s/he usually does not incorporate themselves in public rituals.

## OBA

She is one of the wives of Xangô. A mature woman who can be seductive and passionate, she was so attached to her husband that she spared no effort in trying to hold onto him. It was through this that she fell into the trap of Oshun, who taught her the recipe for a delicious dish and promised it would make Xangô love her forever. Therefore, Oba cut off her one of her ears and put it into the dish, securing herself from her rival Oshun. Only Xangô did not like any of this, and resolved to leave Oba, remaining only with Oshun. Oba was so miserable that her tears created a river. After this, she returned to the world, inhabiting the cemeteries and guarded the tombs.

# OTHER ORIXÁS AND ENTITIES

Candomblé believers are always cautious when Oba and Oshun come together in the same place, as they are known to fight with each other. Oba is a type of dependent woman who will forget herself to secure a man. It is accepted that the lessons of this Orixá emphasize the importance of true love. In nature, Oba is water found in the ponds and lakes.

## EWÁ (IYEWA)

Ewá is also a divinity of the waters and very little is known of her in Brazil. Legend has it that she was a beautiful princess, the preferred daughter of Odùduwà. She lived as a recluse in her castle until Xangô, hoping to win a bet, invaded her retreat to seduce her. Because of her naiveté, she fell suddenly in love with the intruder, who was false in his affections; so, she pleaded that they send her to a place where no other man would ever enter.

Her father therefore sent her to live in the cemetery, where she aged without losing her virginity. In Cuba, Ewá is an old virgin woman who, living in the cemeteries, is responsible for bringing the corpses to Oya.

This Orixá, in the version presented by the researcher Natalia Bolìvar Aróstegui, reveals that the total refusal of ordinary or mundane aspects of life carries certain pessimism about the dangers of carnal pleasures.


OLOKUN

In Africa, they consider Olokun the divinity of the ocean, and Iemanjá a divinity of sweet waters. In Brazil, however, Olokun is female, and credited as being the mother of Iemanjá. As her daughter is now associated with shallow water, Olokun became associated with the deep ocean, where there is no light or sun—that is, the profound abyss where the water and the fire of the earth meet once they have escaped the lava. It is the habitat of strange plants, which have an energy system different from that of all of the other forms of plant life, which depend on photosynthesis.

*Olokun masquerades in Lagos, Nigeria.*

The Cuban legends give various motives that could have led Olokun to hide in the depths of the ocean. Olokun has been in existence ever since the beginning of the world, and had arduous disputes for the domination of the earth. All the stories say that the Orixá was an entity with an indefinable appearance: amphibious, a hermaphrodite that was half-man, half-fish, a mermaid, or even a great underwater serpent. It is said that alone, he/she managed Iemanjá and the waves that worked for her. His/her personality is mysterious and threatening, and some believe that Olokun remains tied to the bottom of the ocean in order to avoid destroying the world. Olokun gives to us the unfathomable depths of collective unconscious wherein, profoundly, the prehistory of humanity hides the true memories of our antecedent species.

OKÔ

Okô is the earth, a masculine Orixá, husband of Olokun, and little known in Brazil. Okô is very serious and chaste. It is said that he is the judge of all disputes, particularly those among women. Okô always arrives at the right decision. He is known to protect all priests that guard the seven keys in the dark interior of the earth. He is the patron of agriculture and of fertilization, and for these reasons women who experience difficulties conceiving can turn to him. When someone dies, Oya brings the corpse to Okô, who will devour it, transforming the fragments of the dead into a source of new life.

## EGUN AND EGUNGUN

In accordance with the Nagô tradition, ancestors can return to earth in certain rituals. The souls of these ancestors are called Egun or Egungun. In Africa, there exist secret societies, composed of only men or only women, who venerate the Egungun.

In Brazil, one of the few secret societies in existence today, run by men, is on the island of Itaparica, called Terreiro de Baba Iliquiobe. During their ceremonies, spirits of the dead appear with layers of cloth covering their entire body so the human form is barely visible. They cannot be touched, so no one will discover what exists beneath these clothes. The secret is fundamental in the religious practices associated with the Egungun. Joana Elbein dos Santos explains why the Egungun is exclusively composed of male spirits: "Historically, in the Yorùbá religion, one of the functions of the groups of Egungun was the denomination 'hunt the Aje' also known by the name *Iya-mi* (literally, our Mothers) or *Iya-agba* (literally, old and veteran Mothers). While at the same time Aje represents the collective image of maternity, fertility, and the quintessential life, as well as representing the persecuted, dominated and aggressive image that can also be female. In this ritual, the strong matriarchal remains of the Yorùbá society are balanced by the male activity of the Egungun. In a distant past, the society of Egungun also had the purpose to discover, punish or banish the old who used this power in a destructive way."[16]

Oya is the only Orixá who appears in the society of the Egungun, since she controls the world of death. According to Yorùbá legends, she also founded the society: only later was it overtaken by the men, who continue to venerate it.

# PART III

# THE DIVINATION SYSTEM OF IFÁ

## THE TRADITION OF IFÁ

In Nigeria, one hour from the city of Lagos, the city of Ode-Remo (state of Ogun) remains one of the most important centers for the religious practices associated with Ifá—the system of Yorùbá divination closely related to the Orixá Ọrúnmìlà and its vast oral corpus consisting of 256 chapters (Odù Ifá). The Yorùbá state is divided into sixteen provinces, corresponding to the sixteen Odù (represented by sixteen palm nuts with "odd" and "even" sides each, totaling 256 combinations) of Ifá still present today, in spite of the great majority of inhabitants who have converted to Christianity or Islam. The old *babalawos* of Ifá are considered to belong to the lineage of ancient priest warriors, and many legends exist with respect to their participation in the resistance against British invasion and colonization. Despite the fact that in modern-day Nigeria the growth of Ifá is a religion in itself, a large portion of the population takes a more prejudicial view, associating it with the "primitiveness" of the past.

To explore this social context, we can consider the experiences of Awo Falokun Fatunmbi, who spoke of his process of initiation into Ifá in Africa. Many people go there seeking to be initiated, but the majority return from there without fulfilling their objectives. Before embarking for Nigeria, Awo had already completed the first stage of initiation with a priest of Ifá whilst in the United States. The secondary stage of the initiation journey in Africa proved more difficult, as it took considerable effort for him to arrive at his destination city, Ode-Remo. He knew that to become initiated he needed to have authorization from the descendants of the royal family of the state of Ogun, as they were the ones who could open the doors of Ifá for him. A simple bracelet that he wore permitted him to meet with his master; he used this when the manager of post office (the local authority to whom he was directed) hesitated to guide him to the house of Oba, a superior priest of Ifá. Awo succeeded only when the post office manager recognized the color and shape of his bracelet on his left wrist—yellow and green, the colors of Ifá—and remarked, "This is your signal." This bracelet was given to him by the North American priest, who predicted, during a consultation, that he too would be a priest of Ifá.

In the passage below, Awo Falokun Fatunmbi explains in detail his meeting with the priest of Ifá during his initiation:

> When the Oluwo returned to the bedroom, he was wet from having taken a bath. His farming clothes had been replaced by a white toga that was wrapped loosely around one shoulder. Using a translator, I told Oluwo that I had come to Africa in hopes of receiving initiation into Ifá. Nodding his head in approval, he picked up a bamboo mat and unrolled it across the floor. He sat on the mat and reached under the bed here he retrieved an old leather briefcase. Carefully he removed his tools of divination from the case.[17]

There was a small divination tray called Opon Ifá, a bag of sacred palm nuts called *ikin*, a bag of yellow powder (from the Irosun tree) called *iyerosun*, and a tapper instrument called *iroke Ifá*. These ceremonial tools are the foundation of all the rituals that occur in traditional Yorùbá religion. The Opon Ifá represents the

Womb of Creation, the *iroke Ifá* is the virility of manifestation, the *ikin* are the fruit of the trees of wisdom and the *iyerosun* is the medicine of transformation. These receptacles of spiritual power are used in conjunction with herbs and prayer (*ọfọ àṣẹ*) to invoke spiritual forces that are used for cleaning, healing, initiation and divination.

The oral tradition of Ifá is based on the teachings of Ọrúnmìlà. In the ancient stories of Ifá, Ọrúnmìlà is described as a Yorùbá man who came to the sacred city of Ile Ifé to teach the system of ethics, religious creation, and mystic vision. At the end of his life, Ọrúnmìlà taught the method of divination, through the casting of sixteen *ikin* (sacred palm nuts), known as *Dafa*. The oral story indicates that Ọrúnmìlà traveled across Africa, spreading his knowledge to other cultures. It is evident that the sacred scriptures of Ifá had enormous influence over the formation of the Yorùbá tradition. We can also see elements of Ifá in the old area of the gulf of Benin.

It is difficult to give a precise date for when Ọrúnmìlà arrived in West Africa. There exists a belief that Ọrúnmìlà previously traveled to Palestine and was known under the name Melquizendeque. Some researchers point towards the similarity between the divination system of Ifá and the oracle of the Essenes, given that both of them are based on the same 256 signs used to catalogue all the forces of nature. Some historians also offer the hypothesis of the associations between the tradition of Ifá and the tradition of the Mystic Eye, which was central to the process of the divination in ancient Egypt. The more elderly Ifá believers argue that they are practicing a religion that originated with the first humans on the earth. Given that human life originated in

Africa, then it is very possible that this notion has roots in specific historical events.

In Brazil, the tradition of Ifá was not preserved in its original form. The *babalawo*, a supreme priest, was replaced as the leader of the Candomblé *terreiro*. While originally only men could work with Ifá consultation, in the Candomblé of Salvador and consequently in the rest of the country the new leaders could be male priest (*pai-de-santo*) or female priestess (*mãe-de-santo*), and acquired the function of *babalawo*. A similar system less known in Africa using cowrie shells (*búzios*) was adopted in Brazil, and the name of the consultation, instead of Ifá, became *jogo de búzios*.

# FROM IFÁ TO JOGO DE BÚZIOS

Once initiated into the Candomblé religion, it is held that beginners should try to reach a state of being that is called *iwa-pelé*. A common translation of *iwa-pelé* would be "softness," although this translation does not express the deep implication that is understood within a religious community of Ifá.

*Iwa-pelé* is the combination of the words *iwa* and *opèlé*. *Iwa* signifies "character," an important word for the Yorùbá people given that personal contribution to the community is mediated in large part by qualities of good character exhibited by the individual in their everyday life. The word *opèlé* means both a woman of Ọrúnmìlà and an instrument used in the divination. The priests of Ifá who express the qualities of *iwa-pelé* are seen as maintaining a balance between the male and female elements of their own character; this balance happens in accordance with the principles found in the scriptures of Ifá. The initiate of Ifá, who fights to be guided by the true meaning of *iwa-pelé*, could gain the right to be called *babalawo*. The word *babalawo* means "father of secrets": *baba* is a Yorùbá word for "father," and *awo* is a word for the "secrets" that are revealed through divination.

The practice of *opelé-Ifá* did not become popular in Bahia. In reality, there existed few *babalawos* in Salvador initiated into Ifá in Africa. In addition, of these, only some occupied places in the hierarchy of the *terreiros* found in the Candomblés of Bahia. It is not possible to specify when the Candomblé priests and priestesses began to give consultations by themselves, employing parts of the original structure from Ifá, trading the original sixteen palm nuts for the sixteen cowrie shells (*búzios*) and assuming for themselves the names and functions of the ancient African *babalawo*. Julio Braga, in his book *O Jogo de Búzios*, attributed these changes to the fact that the original divination practice is intrinsically attached to African society and culture. He says,

> The carriers of this knowledge (culture) arrived here under the condition of captive individuals in Brazil, conditions that were not favorable for the exercise of their functions. The activity of a *babalawo* requires constant practice of divination to enable constant awareness and revelation of their knowledge, something that was only possible within the sociocultural dynamic of society wherein they are originated. We know that the African culture, imported through the process of slavery, was redefined in Brazil wherein it made contact with other cultures, which also joined in the process of creating a new civilization.[18]

Braga concluded that the changes occurred because the *opelé-Ifá* required permanent contact with collective memory, which stores the pertinent mythology of the Odù and their ways, something that proved to be impossible in Brazil, given that the cultural context is quite different. Therefore, there would have to be a process of reinterpretation of the myths, adapting them to their new Brazilian environment. Through this, they created a model that uses a long process of initiation and is easier to operate.

## DAFA: CONSULTING THE DIVINATION SYSTEM OF IFÁ

The initiation of Ifá priests is extremely complex; it is a tradition recycled periodically through the meetings promoted by the ancient councils in Yorùbáland, enabling the *babalawos* to transmit the tradition of Ifá.

The consultation of Ifá it called *Ifá dida*, while the process of casting the sixteen *ikin* (*coco-de-dende*) is called *dafa*. The *babalawo* takes all of the *ikin* at once, shakes them in his hands from left to right, whilst singing prayers (*ọfọ àṣẹ*). When the *ikin* are in his left hand, he takes as much as he can out with his right hand. If he keeps two *ikin* in his left hand, he forms one vertical mark (I) on the floor with his indicating finger. If there is only one *ikin* placed in his hand, he will make two vertical marks on the floor (II). When there is more than two *ikin* left, or when there is none placed in his left hand, he will not make a mark and so the process starts again. In accordance with the throws made, he draws the marks, one beneath the other. The *babalawo* repeats this process four times. For example:

>   I
>  II
>  II
>  II

This column, called the "leg" of the Odù, is reproduced by the *babalawo*, who draws for each two identical "legs" that indicate the twin legs (*meji*) of the Odù:

```
   II
  IIII
  IIII
  IIII
```

A single line represents the line of expansion in the universe, and a double line represents the force of contraction. One author explains the matter this way:

> In metaphysical terms, expansion manifests as light, and contraction manifests as darkness. Within the cosmology of Ifá, darkness and light create all that there is. It is an expression of the idea that light contradicts to become matter and that matter dissolves into light. In Taoism, this polarity is symbolized by a circle filled with a black and white teardrop called 'yin' and 'yang.' Neither Taoism nor Ifá considers light to be 'good' or dark to be 'evil.' Dark and light, expansion and contraction, are simply two manifestations of a single form of spiritual substance that emanates from [a cosmic] source.[19]

Therefore, *dafa* is a graphic representation of the ways in which light and darkness are integrated within the formation of the universe. The divination literature of Ifá is also divided into sixteen parts (sixteen Odù) and every Odù has a specific Yorùbá name. To hear the verses is like entering into contact with a real voice that shares discoveries and experiences with a consultant. The casting of Odù in the *jogo de búzios* determines which Odù is predominant at that moment. In the "game" of *búzios* in Brazil, we lost part of this tradition, although the names of the Odù are still almost the same.

Below, we see a "map" (of the sixteen principal Ifá Odù) with the marks and the respective Odù, recorded by Pierre Verger and Roger Bastide:

1
OGBÊ-MEJI OR EJI-OGBÊ
I I
I I
I I
I I

2
OYẸKU-MEJI
II II
II II
II II
II II

3
IWORI-MEJI
II II
I I
I I
II II

4
ODI-MEJI
I I
II II
II II
I I

5
IROSUN-MEJI
I I
I I
II II
II II

6
OWONRIN-MEJI
II II
II II
I I
I I

7
ỌBARA-MEJI
I I
II II
II II
II II

8
ỌKANRAN-MEJI
II II
II II
II II
I I

9
OGUMDA-MEJI
I I
I I
I I
II II

## 10
## ỌSA-MEJI
II II
I I
I I
I I

## 11
## IKA-MEJI
II II
I I
II II
II II

## 12
## OTURUPON-MEJI
II II
II II
I I
II II

## 13
## OTURA-MEJI
I I
II II
I I
I I

## 14
### IRẸTẸ-MEJI

I I
I I
II II
I I

## 15
### ỌSẸ-MEJI

I I
II II
I I
II II

## 16
### OFUN-MEJI

II II
I I
II II
I I

The light and dark duality, the masculine and feminine principle, is defined in the cowrie shells of the *jogo de búzios* in the form of "closed" and "open" ones. The *búzios* (cowrie shells) are specially prepared by cutting the bottom part. The side where there exists a natural split is considered closed, and the other, whose surface was broken, is considered the open part. There are always sixteen cowrie shells used in the "game."

| COMBINATIONS | | DIVINITIES |
|---|---|---|
| *Open* | *Closed* | |
| 1 | 15 | Exu |
| 2 | 14 | Ibeji |
| 3 | 13 | Ogum/Iemanjá |
| 4 | 12 | Oxóssi |
| 5 | 11 | Oxum/Ewá/Iemanjá |
| 6 | 10 | Xangô |
| 7 | 9 | Exu |
| 8 | 8 | Obàtálá |
| 7 | 7 | Oya/Egun |
| 10 | 6 | Obàtálá |
| 11 | 5 | Exu |
| 12 | 4 | Xangô |
| 13 | 3 | Omolu/Nanã/Oshunmare |
| 14 | 2 | Egun |

The *opelé-Ifá* is another divination system used in Africa and in Cuba, also known as *colar* or *rosario* (prayer beads) of Ifá. Mango seeds, with sides well differentiated by color, are placed in a chain and held together in a row, in the number eight or sixteen. At one time, the throw is repeated four times until they complete the drawing of the *Odù* (as is the case used with *ikin*) with the *rosario*; the *babalawo* verifies which *Odù* has responded to his question, after only one toss. This kind of consultation does not exist in Brazil, although it is very well known in Cuba; in Brazil the Ifá consultation has been reduced almost exclusively to the *jogo de búzios*. The relative simplicity of the *jogo de búzios* in comparison to the consultation of Ifá, and the absence of the self-regulating communities such as those found in Africa, produce an enormous variety of readings related to the casting of cowrie shells and the interpretations of the Odù by the Brazilian *babalawo*.

In the *jogo de búzios*, the *babalawo* asks, in one of the castings, which Orixá is responding. There are discrepancies between the Candomblé of different houses (*terreiros*) in other Brazilian states, in relation to how the casting of the cowrie shells correspond to them. We are opting here for the type examined by Julio Braga in his book, *Jogo de Búzios*.

Generally, after the consultation, the *babalawo* prescribes an *ebó* (ritual sacrifice or offering), which should be done to strengthen the Odù of a person, or to please one of the Orixás in charge of the specific consultation, in remuneration for the graces attained. According the tradition, initially, the *babalawo* does not ask anything about the life of the client; at the end of the consultation, they verify anything the client wants to understand in more detail or ask if there are specific questions not sufficiently answered. There are several ways in which each *babalawo* "plays," including how the *babalawo* arranges the divining table and their tools. Some use a candle; others use a crystal and a variety of other amulets. There exists no consensus. If the client does not frequent the *terreiro*, it is usual for them to pay for the session in cash, which can be put toward the community's daily expenses.

# PART IV

## THE RITUAL: THE ORIXÁS DRINK, EAT, AND DANCE

## TRANCE AND INITIATION

When someone goes to a Candomblé ceremony and begins to feel disorientated or lose their senses, that person is said to be *bola*, the Orixá's calling. The trance of the Orixá, however, does not occur suddenly or in any given place; it happens because of the process of initiation and is considered the goal of any "daughter" or "son" of the Orixá because of the close contact with the divinity.[20] It is very rare that this meeting should happen without a process of long and careful preparation. The phenomenon of an encounter with an Orixá is something that takes over the individual little by little, across a long process of apprenticeship in the *terreiro*, participating in the rituals, and observing the commandments and teachings transmitted orally by the priests or priestesses.

The trance in Candomblé has nothing to do with the incorporation of ancestral spirits, who feel an urgency to communicate with the world of the living like those that occur in Umbanda and in Spiritualism in Brazil. The initiation includes a period of reclusion in which the *yawo/iawos* (daughters of the Orixás) and the *omorissa/omorixas* (sons of the Orixás) receive a rigorous training, making them able to reach a state of purity that is necessary for the Orixá to come to the earth. The new members of the *terreiro* must also learn the dance steps of the divinities and their principal tradition. Here it is important to explain the festivities and performance in the public celebrations of Candomblé: "Every ceremony is a religious representation in which actors and spectators participate. On the return of an Orixá to the earth, ritual clothing and emblems are brought to dress the initiated whilst in the trance; the rhythms, the songs and the choreography perpetuate myths, which constitute a precious heritage transmitted from generation to generation by the *iawo*. It is the patrimony of the community."[21]

According to Gisele Cossard, the *iawo* will permit—through her being—"the [Orixá] to come"; it will be a personality of his/her "Orixá of the head" (principal Orixá that guides the "head" of a person) and become more articulated within him/her. "It corresponds to the archetype but will acquire the nuances in accordance with every individual. Little by little, the Orixás acquire the power of speech, and with time and experience it is possible for them to develop signs of personal knowledge: double vision, prophecy, secret language, knowledge of plants, remedies, etc."[22]

The life of an *iawo* is governed by the same philosophy that orientates the Orixá, and the familiarity comes to be seen as a second personality, as the *iawo*'s double. In this intimate contact between the initiated and the divinity, the person receives, alongside the energetic aura of the Orixá, revelations of their own unconscious energy, which can let blossom aspects of their life in a harmonious and rejuvenating way.

The *iawo* generally receives one or two Orixás. The first one is called the "Orixá of the head" and the other, secondary one encompasses aspects of the individual personality of the medium. Usually, the Candomblé priest or priestess reads which Orixá is manifesting and to which ancestral family he/she belongs. This reading can be made alongside a consultation of Ifá, or observing the way the trance occurs during specific songs for this or that Orixá. Monique Augras called attention to another aspect in her reading of Orixá manifestation:

> All of these divinities, of origin, of heritage, of destiny, congregate themselves in the individual, revealing determined configurations, so complex and so dynamic that they are called '*enredo*'—a term which signifies the story containing a series of complexities. The '*enredo*' of one piece is the intrigue, which animates the characters and directions of action. The individual is placed at the center of a divine drama, where the leader of the head expresses himself/herself in the first place because he/she has settled for the rights of the initiation. In addition, the process of initiation has the function to set down equally all of the divinities of the '*enredo*' in their respective places. In this way, all of the relations between these divinities can be shared in the most harmonious way. It is often said that both the second and the third Orixá of the head can have powerful influence. The responsibility in short of the high priestess or priest affirmed by this work consists in placing every one of the divinities of '*enredo*' in the place where they belong.[23]

The first ritual of initiation is the *bori*, or "offering for the head." The *bori* composes itself through a sequence of rituals, which start with ceremonies for the purification of the body such as baths prepared with special herbs. The apprentice remains in the *camarinha* or *rondaime*, lying down on a straw mat covered with a white sheet or blanket, communicating only with the Candomblé priest or priestess. On the day preceding the principal ritual, they keep to a special diet, eating only very light food in accordance with the tradition. Afterwards, ritual food is provided in the form of one (or two) sacrificed pigeons and an offering of fruits cakes and flowers for the head (*ori*) of the initiate. This feast is afterwards offered to the members of the community who had partaken in the ritual the night before. The morning after the ritual, the head of the initiate is washed; this ritual is called the "cleansing of the beaded necklace" of the "Orixá of the head" belonging to the initiated, alongside the beads belonging to the Orixá of the house (*terreiro*).

The principal ritual of initiation is called "the confirmation." It consists of an act of shaving and painting the head, much more complex than the *bori*, with a period of withdrawal lasting multiple days and a process of divination much longer and more detailed. Knowledge of the proceedings, which are involved in these rituals, is reserved only for the initiated. The rituals happen according to the *enredo* (narrative plot) of the initiated and his or her Orixás are set down in recipient containers made of clay, china, or wood to collect objects that represent the specific characteristics of the African divinities; examples include stones, shells, and pieces of iron and other natural elements. In order to consecrate this recipient, which will be called the Orixá itself, the blood of the animals is offered. Parallel to this step the Orixá is set down symbolically over the head of the initiated. This ritual is called to "shave" or "make the head"; if they are collective, they are called "a boat." The process culminates in a great celebration, dominated by *saída de iyawo* or *saida do barco* ("departure of the boat"); the boat refers to all of the initiates who were formed at the same time.

A public ceremony of Candomblé generally happens within the space called *barracão* (big tent) or simply the *terreiro* "ground," which involves, in a repetitive and sequential presentation, a diverse range of traditional drumming, singing, dancing, and performances of stories and proverbs. Several languages could be used according the origin of the Candomblé house: Jeje, Yorùbá, Kikongo, or Kimbundu—the last ones, usually in the minority, come from Bantu Africa and are sometimes mixed with Portuguese. Among the mediums and helpers (*ogan* and *ekedi*) are people from across society—bricklayers, domestic house cleaners, tailors, teachers, workers, soldiers, police officers, lawyers—all of whom respond by same name, "brothers and sisters." In the arena of the *terreiro*, they perform a collective mythology according to their own spiritual "plots" for each Orixá incorporated by the *iyawo*. They are brought together by the sacred archetypes that respond to the first call from the beating of drums, followed by songs that allude to the heroic deeds and great transformations performed by African divinities while living among humans. The sound penetrates and illuminates the body with rhythmical movements, while the voice of the master of ceremonies and the ritual chorus describe in an epic manner aspects of the life of each Orixá or Vodun. They generally target the body possessed by the Orixá, leading a choreographed set of movements spread across the Candomblé sacred ground like a mythology reenacted by the performance.

The Orixá awakens. Since the most important moment for the Orixá is the dance, everybody who belongs to the religion becomes a potential dancer. The strong connection with the Orixá is found within the barefoot dance of the incorporated medium. It is through the barefoot that energy takes hold of the entire body in a kind of ecstasy, repeating traditional choreographies for each Orixá in a personal and unique way. Whilst they may say that the Orixá comes down to the earth, when we consider this action we can observe how the Orixá springs up from the earth, like a strong light, illuminating the whole body.

Once the Orixá possesses the initiated, they are brought to the interior of the house to be adorned with particular clothing, a dress gala to the Orixá who came that day. Moreover, when it is time for the music of the Orixá, he/she enters holding his/her true adornment and objects, maneuvering around the center of the *terreiro* and dancing according to the proper and traditional song. The persona of the initiated disappears when they are dressed up as ancient kings or queens belonging to an idealized African ancestral time. When observed more closely, it is interesting that what we have is in fact a composite costume: African fabrics with stamping, mixed sometimes with cotton or calico, with French lace and synthetic Chinese silk.

In several cases, individual awareness does not disappear completely. Personal consciousness is not eliminated through the trance; rather, it is brought to life together with the sacred function of acting in a divine spectacle. In this other theatre, once the actor grasps the mask, he removes his social role revealing his/her true self as the most sacred part of the human being.

### EBÓ: FOOD FOR THE ORIXÁS

Ebó is a term originating from the Yorùbá language that means in the general sense "sacrifice or offering to the Orixá." Some Candomblés use the word only when referring to sacrifices of animals, but it can be given a more inclusive meaning, referring

# TRANCE AND INITIATION

also to the offerings of vegetables, fruits, flowers, and various objects. In Umbanda, it is common to encounter the word *ebó* exclusively referring to offerings for Exu, which are placed on crossroads and popularly called *despachos* (dispatches).

The *ebó* has great importance in the religion of the Orixás. *Arriar um ebó* (to lay down an *ebó*) is a ritualistic action, a detailed process of approximation and exchange with an Orixá. Before anything, we must consult the *búzios* through an *iyalorixá* (priestess) or *babalorixá* (priest) to have the first contact with the divinities. In the *jogo do búzios*, the Orixá speaks about the physical, mental, and spiritual life of the client, and it points out which offerings are needed to promote health and personal balance. If the person needs the help of a specific Orixá to reach his goal, the positive response from the divinity comes through the request of *ebó*; the client is also informed about the place and the time in which the offering will be better appreciated by the Orixá in charge of the quest.

After this comes the stage of choosing and acquiring the foods and gifts that will compose the *ebó*. Following this, the plates of food that are more complex (if there are any) must be prepared by someone qualified for this task within the Candomblé house. This person then comes to a specific place, which would be in an open space or within the house of the Orixá, and finally *arria o ebó* (lay down the *ebó*). It is fundamental that in this moment the person concentrates upon the object they are offering as *ebó*; they express to the Orixá their desire, need, or their gratitude.

Candomblé gives a lot of value to the work involved in choosing and putting together small things, preparing ingredients for food, and fulfilling tasks such as entering the forest to deposit flowers on the margins of a waterfall or laying down something for Exu. *Arriar um ebó* is to perpetrate a trade with Axé (the sacred force) between the two worlds, the sacred (*Orum*) and the profane (*Aye*). This is because in the religion of the Orixás, it is believed that everything in existence has an aspect of Axé. People, animals, vegetables, minerals, and any other object all have an affinity with one of the Orixás, and the energy must always remain in motion between the visible, material, profane world and the invisible, astral, sacred one. Such as the cycle of waters, always flowing from one place to another, guarantees life on earth through successive rain, evaporation, cooling, and thawing, in Candomblé the dynamic of the transferences of Axé is an essential part of life.

Since colonial times in Brazil, the *ebós* have also been a preferred point of attack for opponents of Candomblé. The preconception spread by the official culture contributed to a distorted vision of the Candomblé rituals and philosophy. It is perhaps unfair that in today's culture, wherein we benefit from a growth in ecological awareness and more information available to the public, the followers of Candomblé are still unjustly accused of environmental predation. In reality, the sacrificed animals in the *terreiros* also serve as food for the community, and the glass vessels, bottles, and dishwater are cleaned and recycled. In such a time when the religion of the Orixás becomes better known and more respected, we will learn that any devotee can recycle the *ebós* left in outside places. When this happens, perhaps we will understand why the devastation in the forest, or the pollution in rivers and seas, threatens the survival of Candomblé; or even more important, ecologists and environmental educators will pay attention to how this ancient religion (once called "primitive") is still alive today and continues to venerate the forces of nature.

Often when living in cities, people forget that the beef with onions laid on the table came from an innocent calf, killed by human beings to feed other individuals of the same species. The same applies to a thigh of chicken, or a filet of fish, or even vegetables that arrive green in the stomach, which were once cut and pulled from the earth. However, in Candomblé, which venerates the ancestors and forces of nature, the sacrifice of animals is sacred, and their death is comprehended as a true transformation, an inseparable part of their own life.

# SACRED SPACES OF CANDOMBLÉ

The internal space in Candomblé communities has a specific configuration, which is left many times varied, in the disposition of the *quartinhos*—small rooms where the shrines of the Orixás reside. Generally, in the entrance and exit, there is a room or "house of Exu." Usually it is closed, and only opened on ritual occasions, including offerings. It is common for a statue or symbol of Exu's presence to be in the door of his house.

Once you enter the *terreiro*, you can sometimes see the rooms of the other Orixás, always with the doors closed. They can be placed in circles or in lines, side by side. Inside of every room, there are the *peji*, the altars of the Orixás where there are the *ota*, sacred stones where they have "settled" their respective Axé. The *ota* of every Orixá is found inside a special vessel of china or clay, preserved in palm oil or honey, alongside other substances. It is the rooms that the votive offerings are placed. In the past, during the time when Candomblé was persecuted, it was common for there to be a large table full of Catholic saints within these rooms. In the lower part, disguised, hidden by a big white cloth, would be the Orixá's settlement.

In the indoor patio of the *terreiros,* it is very common to find trees and sacred plants connecting the Axé with the Orixás: the floss-silk of Oxóssi, the palm oil tree of Exu and Ifá, the Orixá Iroko. We also see natural fountains, artificial lakes or wells. The presence of water is very important. The largest constructed part is generally a large covered area, which must be high with good ventilation, sometimes without outer walls, localized where most of the rituals and public ceremonies happen. Near this structure, there is situated the *camarinha*, a preparation room to dress up the Orixás that serves as a theatrical green room wherein the Orixás are ornamented. In some *terreiros*, the reclusion area that is reserved for the initiated is called *rondaime*.

The kitchen is another space extremely important in all Candomblé *terreiros*. It is there that the devotees prepare foods for the *filhos de casa* (children of the house) and the offerings in the form of delicious dishes to please the appetite of the Orixás. Before they light the fire, the ingredients are carefully chopped up by the *iawos* into specific shapes and sizes and, during the cooking, the visual disposition of more complex dishes is personally supervised by the *iyalorixá*, who has a acute aesthetic sense, combining sight, smell, and taste to better please their living divinities. The kitchen is also a good meeting place, since it is a hub of activity. Therein, much conversation about the preferred food of the divinities, myths, and traditions of Candomblé occurs.

Whilst in Brazil, Candomblé benefits from many possibilities of space both outside and inside. In New York, a city of crowded concrete buildings, the devotees of Lukumí or Santeria (adopted names for the Orixá religion imported from Cuba) redefined the question of sacred space. A good explanation of this is offered by *babalawo* John Mason through an interview with the author:

> When you came into my house some minutes ago,
> you passed by a shrine. You never saw it. Every
> house we got that there are Yorùbá people inside,
> they have a shrine to Elegba [Exu] at the front
> door. Most people don't see it. They pass by it. That
> space is a dedicated one, a sacred space, more or

less, bigger or smaller. A woman once told me, 'I have to rent an apartment; I need three bedrooms.' Why three bedrooms? 'One for my son, one for me and the other for my Orisha.' That indicated the way that people think when they are part of this culture. But the Orishas also become individuals. They take the place of human beings. They become family. They share the space with you. It is not something separate from you. So this is maybe the one strength that keeps us from being Catholic or Protestant. We do not place them somewhere [and] just go visit. They will never leave this house. We might have a temple. There will be a space for all of us, but mine is always upstairs, or at my door or downstairs or in my yard, so that my relation to Divinity is always close at hand and becomes part of my living space. They are not outside my space. It is not something outside; it is every space. Its people who wear *eleke* (beaded necklaces). You wear it around your neck; it takes up your body. They wear bracelets, etc. It is the clothes you wear. All of this is ritual space. Your body is a temple. To get technical, your body becomes ritual place that is designed; your design is what you wear.[24]

## RELIGION, LIFE, AND ART

In every *peji* there is a unique atmosphere, which can provoke something special and personal in every one of us. Every priest nourishes the Orixás in an extremely particular way. When we enter the sacred space of a *peji*, we also enter an intimate space; we see the traces of blood from the sacrifices and breathe the same air as the Orixás. We come across everyday objects scattered about the place, such as objects with supermarket logos, articles that belong to "consumer society," bottles, and cheap porcelain vases that are placed alongside sacred stones, always protected, shrouded from our inquiring eye. In rare cases, in some less orthodox Candomblé communities, we find alongside this congregation of apparently conflicting elements images of Christian saints, which lends a softer aspect to the chaos of colors and objects. At times, we might look upon these facts as being the end of the Candomblé tradition, yet we can also see this more as an expression of its resistance, its fortification, and its endless capacity, in addition to the sacrifice given to us by nature.

Whilst the tradition of Candomblé continues to be transmitted orally, we should not ignore how the religion is now also being spread by the infinite publications, images, and videos found on hundreds of websites—something unheard of when I first published this book. It is known that the first Candomblé houses in Bahia were founded and organized by ex-captive individuals who had been made priests in the ancient kingdoms of Dahomey, Ketu, or Oyo. Leaders at that time led their descendants to the maximum number of posts in the first Candomblé, who today still exercise hierarchical power over the new *terreiros* that have been founded in the outer regions of Brazil. This rigid hierarchy is responsible for maintaining the basic principles of the religion. Relying on the oral transmission of knowledge, the *iawo* learns to observe and hear his masters. Still, however, there is a degree to which the rituals are perpetuated by the network of communication based around those who live together as followers from all social classes.

The African masters, who were children of the Orixás and who came to Salvador from African lands, brought with them the foundational cultural understandings that became Candomblé. The drastic environmental changes we have experienced such as the destruction of tropical forests together with rise of great urban centers and socioeconomic oppression have in some ways managed to transform attitudes to Candomblé, which was always a focus of black cultural resistance. During the Brazilian military dictatorship, many researchers who were persecuted during the regime encountered in Candomblé new forms of resistance: passive militancy and humanity. In recent years, Candomblé is active in the political life of the country for half of its leading religions, supporting movements against social injustice, and all the prejudices that still afflict us all.

National artists of Bahia, and many other Bahians for that matter, enter into this culture, transforming it into a synonym for Afro-Brazil. Masterpieces have emerged, but in many cases, the work of the author is ignored. Candomblé is still seen as folklore, and is a recurrent theme in numerous caricatures of the Afro-Brazilian religion in Carnival; the way in which it appears in carnival belittles its cultural strength, given that there is still little truly known about it aside from Brazilian media stereotypes.

The art of Candomblé liturgy has always been committed to maintaining the tradition. However, in the desire to continue to create beautiful and sacred altars that demonstrate to the Orixá they venerate, they often invest in contemporary materials. The result sometimes appears on altars that differ greatly from those altars for the Orixás in Africa, because they also include elements of modern culture such as plastic objects bought in supermarkets or malls. The imagination can sometimes synchronize with the deep feeling that is the Orixá and transcend contact with the Candomblé priest in charge of preserving the truly African tradition, inspiring the person in charge of the Candomblé altar to innovate within the faith and to transform everyday objects into alter elements of very ancient ancestors.

## NEW AND OLD PATHS

The *peji* or altars of the Orixá are solemnly impressive. Each one has its unique history and atmosphere. Each Candomblé priest feeds his/her Orixá in an extremely personal way. When we approach the *peji*, we are entering a very intimate, sacred space. The *peji* is the banqueting table on which the feast for the Orixá is spread out.

Besides the scared stones (which are always covered from inquisitive gaze), we notice items of daily use, taken from the shelves of any common refrigerator—objects form the "consumer society" like bottles and ceramic vases. The presence of religious statues lends a mildly ascetic aura to the combination of unusual shapes and colors. Instead of viewing this mixture as a sign of the degeneration of Candomblé traditions, we should understand it as a manifestation of creative cultural resistance: Candomblé's tireless capacity to make anything a sacred object.

The tradition of Candomblé was once transmitted orally from the old Yorùbá and Dahomey kingdoms. Throughout Brazil and neighboring countries, this hierarchical network of communication spread ritual knowledge and practices that preserve the Orixá. Nowadays there are adepts in all classes of society, even though the majority of those who practice this religion are from poor and humble backgrounds. Many African teachers have gone away. Drastic changes in human society, the destruction of the rain forest, and socioeconomic oppression have all transformed Candomblé—the center of resistance for black culture in Brazil—into new and misled forms of religious manifestation.

Artists, writers, and musicians born in Salvador—such as Jorge Amado, Dorival Caymmi, Caetano Veloso, Gilberto Gil—as well as many others who are Bahian by choice if not by birth have been steeped in Candomblé culture and traditions. And although great works have been produced by these artists, Candomblé is still viewed a folkloric curiosity by the Brazilian authorities.

Candomblé is not a religion of the masses. You may turn to Candomblé for help, even for miracles. The doors are always open. By crossing the threshold, you are looking for the Creator and the Orixás. Suddenly, you are transported to another place, a very beautiful place. It seems that you have been there before, perhaps in a dream. You wonder why orchards are no longer like this. This place is not just filled with decorations. The trees are so beautiful, most without fruit, although Oxóssi's mango trees are there. Birdcalls and the common grunt of a pig create a rural atmosphere. You relax and look around, feeling that the environment was prepared for your arrival. A friend shared these words with the author. By entering the Candomblé house for the first time, this author had the same feeling about this magical place.

Those who come to frequent Candomblé learn that every day is a new lesson, passed on by those older priests and priestess that teach us. They teach us songs, cultural ways of the Orixás and Voduns or Minkisi, simple ways of living, how to look after oneself and read the divine presence in nature, to pray and to ritualize the moment, to let go of negative memories, and to fortify one's life in the present. We learn how we can best please the divinities; that the last time we looked, they were always found inside of us and this can be revealed by the *bori* initiation, when we offer food for our head (*ori*). In participating in the religion, we discover our mother and father's ancestors, new and ancient parents, and our spiritual families. And from here on we are able to share with other families of Orixás and our brothers and sisters in spirit, each one with their Orixás, Voduns or Minkisi—siblings through rituals, the sound of the *atabaque* (drum), the songs and the heat of the circular or zigzag dance.

We learn also that there are so many qualities belonging to each Orixá—their myths, symbols and appropriate colors—and the many types of music and dances that are appropriate for every occasion, mysteries that we discover by living together. All this knowledge and the questions left to explore make a lifetime seem too short to complete. This long initiation has no end: composed of steps to be met, new doors to open, new paths and searches, and meetings inside and outside ourselves. *Candom-blé*, composed of three syllables, is a difficult and a beautiful word. Even more difficult is understanding how three concepts—religion, life, and art—we often view as separate can be indissolubly bound together by the traditions of the Orixás.

# SELECTED BIBLIOGRAPHY

Aróstegui, Natália Bolívar. *Los Orishas en Cuba*. Havana: Ediciones Unión, 1990.

Augras, Monique. *O Duplo e a Metamorfose - A Identidade Mítica em Comunidades Nagôs*. Petrópolis, Rio de Janeiro: Vozes, 1983.

Bastide, Roger. *A Cozinha dos Deuses: Alimentação e Candomblés*. Rio de Janeiro: Serviço de Alimentação da Previdência Social, 1952.

Bastide, Roger. *O Candomblé da Bahia: Rito Nagô*. São Paulo: Companhia das Letras, 2001.

Binon, Gisèle Cossard. *Contribution a l'étude des Candomblés au Brésil: Le Candomblé Angola*. Ph.D. dissertation, Paris, Sorbonne, 1970.

Binon, Gisèle Cossard. "A Filha-de-Santo," in *Olórrisa, Escritos sobre a Religião dos Orixás*. São Paulo: Agora, 1981.

Braga, Júlio. *O Jogo de Búzios*. São Paulo: Brasiliense, 1988.

Cacciatore, Olga Gudolle. *Dicionário de Cultos Afro-Brasileiros*. Rio de Janeiro: Forense Universitária, 1977.

Carneiro, Edison. *Religiões Negras*. Rio de Janeiro: Editora Civilização Brasileira, 1963.

Carvalho, Cônego José Geraldo Vidigal de. *A Igreja e a Escravidão*. Rio de Janeiro: Presença, 1985.

Chebel, Malek. *L'Esclavage en Terre d'Islam*. Paris: Pluriel, 2007.

Coutinho, D. José Joaquim da Cunha Azeredo. *Concordância das Leis de Portugal e das Bulas Pontificais*. Rio de Janeiro: Arquivo Nacional, 1988.

Fatunmbi, Awo Falokun. *Iwa-pelé: Ifá Quest: The Search for the Source of Santeria and Lucumi*. North Charleston, SC: CreateSpace, 2013.

Landes, Ruth. *Cidade das Mulheres*. Rio de Janeiro: Editora Civilização Brasileira, [1947] 1967.

Ligiéro, Zeca. "Candomblé is Religion-Life-Art," in *Divine Inspiration from Benin to Bahia*. Albuquerque: University of New México Press, 1992.

Lima, Vivaldo Costa. *A Família de Santo nos Candomblés Jeje-Nagôs da Bahia*. Bahia: Editora UFBA, 1977.

Mason, John. *Orin Orísá: Songs for Selected Heads*. New York: Yoruba Theological Archministry, 1992.

Parés, Luis Nicolau. *The Formation of Candomblé: Vodun History and Ritual in Brazil* Chapel Hill: University of North Carolina Press, 2013.

Pierson, Donald. *Brancos e Pretos na Bahia*. São Paulo: Brasiliana, 1971.

Reis, João José. *A Morte é uma Festa: Ritos Fúnebres e Revolta Popular no Brasil do Século XIX*. São Paulo: Companhia das Letras, 1992.

Ramos, Arthur. *O Negro Brasileiro: Etnografia religiosa e psicanálise*. Rio de Janeiro, Civilização Brasileira, 1934.

Rodrigues, Nina. *Os Africanos no Brasil*. São Paulo: Companhia Editora Nacional, 1932.

Santos, Deoscoredes M. dos and Elbein, Juana. "O Culto dos Ancestrais na Bahia: O Culto dos Egun," in *Oloorisa, Escritos sobre a Religião dos Orixás*. São Paulo: Agora, 1981.

Thompson, Robert Farris. *Flash of the Spirit: African and Afro-American Art and Philosophy*. New York: Random House, 1983.

Verger, Pierre. *Orixás*. Salvador, Bahia: Corrupio, 1981.

Verger, Pierre. *Fluxo e Refluxo do Tráfico de Escravos entre o Golfo do Benim e a Bahia de Todos os Santos*. Salvador, Bahia: Corrupio, 1987.

Verger, Pierre. "Contribuição ao Estudo da Adivinhação no Salvador (Bahia)" with Roger Bastide, in *Oloorisa, Escritos sobre a Religião dos Orixás*. São Paulo: Agora, 1981.

# NOTES

1. Pierre Verger, *Notes sur le culte des orisa et vodun...* (Dakar: IFAN, 1957), 385.

2. *Terreiro*: Internal space of Candomblé; a large building or "ground" where the public rituals are performed.

3. R. H. Stone in Robert Farris Thompson, *Flash of the Spirit: African and Afro-American Art and Philosophy* (New York: Vintage Books, 1984), 3.

4. John Mason, *Orin Orisa: Songs for Selected Heads* (New York: Yoruba Theological Archministry, 1992), 3-4.

5. See Pierre Verger, *Fluxo e Refluxo: tráfico dos escravos entre Benin e a Bahia* (Salvador: Corrupio, 2002).

6. Malek Chebel, *L'esclavage en Terre d'Islam: un tabou bien gardé* (Paris: Librairie Arthème Fayard, 2007), 15.

7. A "bull" is special decree that only the Catholic Pope can sign. A "papal bull" is a particular type of letter, patent or charter issued by a Pope of the Catholic Church. These bulls were originally issued by the Pope for many kinds of communication of a public nature, but by the thirteenth century, papal bulls were only used for the most formal or solemn of occasions.

8. Gisele Cossard, *Contribuition a l'etude des candomblés au Brésil: les Candomblé Angola* (Ph.D. dissertation, Paris, Sorbonne, 1970), 38.

9. Pierre Verger, *Notas do culto aos Orixás e Voduns* (Salvador: Corrupio, 1999), 20.

10. Luis Nicolau Parés, *The Formation of Candomblé: Vodun History and Ritual in Brazil.* Chapel Hill: University of North Carolina Press, 2013), 81.

11. Parés, *Candomblé*, 82.

12. Parés, *Candomblé*, 209.

13. The term *caboclo* refers to persons of indigenous and white (Portuguese) parentage.

14. Dorival Caymmi's "Vatapá" was recorded by the band Anjos do Inferno (Columbia, 1942), and by Dorival Caymmi in his *Eu Vou Pra Maracangalha* (Odeon,1957). The lyrics of Caymmi's song describe the complete recipe for preparing the *vatapá*, the famous African-Bahian dish.

15. Awo Falokun Fatunmbi, *Iwa-Pele: Ifa Quest: The Search for the Source of Santeria and Lucumi* (North Charleston, SC: CreateSpace, 2013), 131.

16. See Joana Elbein dos Santos, *Os Nàgô e a Morte Pàde, Àsèsè e o Culto Égun na Bahia* (Petropolis, Rio de Janeiro: Editora Vozes Ltds., 1975).

17. Fatunmbi, *Ifa Quest*, 50.

18. See Júlio Braga, *O Jogo de Búzios: Um Estudo de Adivinhação no Candomblé* (São Paulo: Brasiliense, 1988), 88.

19. Fatunmbi, *Ifa Quest*, 88.

20. When one attends a Candomblé house, she or he receives the name of "Abian." When the neophyte is initiated, s/he then receives the name Omo Orixá (son or daughter of the Orixá). After the first initiation, s/he will be confirmed and go through a ritual called *fazer a cabeça*—making of the head. From there, s/he may receive the Orixá through a trance and will become a true child of the Orixá," or s/he receive a position in the organization of the house as an *ogan* (for men) and or *ekedi* (for women). Both are helpers for all the rituals.

21. See Cossard, *Contribuition a l'etude des candomblés au Brésil*.

22. See Cossard, *Contribuition a l'etude des candomblés au Brésil.*

23. Idem.

24. John Mason, Interview with author, Brooklyn, New York, 1987.

# INDEX

A

Abeokuta   14-15
Africa, imagined   3
African
  cultural groups   16, 19, 23
  cultures   26, 116
  divinities   25, 27, 30, 33, 132-3
  lands   21, 45-6, 144
  myths   57
  origins   3, 30
  religions   5, 9, 19-20, 23-5, 27, 30, 69, 136
Africanization   31
Afro-Brazil (African-Brazilians)   27-9, 31, 144
Afro-Brazilian cultures   1, 3
Afro-Brazilian religion   3, 34, 50, 144
Afro-Brazilian scholars   30
Aja   16, 18, 20
altars   28, 55-6, 139, 145, 147
ancestors   3, 20, 79, 88, 105, 137
Angolan Candomblé   9, 16, 31, 83, 86
animals   41-2, 46, 67-8, 81, 87, 132, 134, 136-7
anointings   28-9
*aracajé*   33
archetype   48, 50, 57-8, 87, 96, 130
Aroni   35
art   14-15, 36, 42, 79, 143, 145, 149

artists   24, 148
*awo*   111-12, 115
Awo Falokun Fatunmbi   41, 111-12
Axé   41-3, 53, 136, 139
Ayguna   47

B

*babalawo* (*babalaô*)   15, 18, 48, 111, 114-17, 124-5
*babalorixá* (priest)   135 *see also* priest
Bahia   18, 23, 26, 28-9, 31, 33, 45, 48-9, 66, 115, 125, 143
Bahians   3, 33-4, 144, 148
Bantu Africa   50, 133
*batuque*   19, 25-7
beaches   6, 53, 55
beads, white   77, 83, 86
boat (Candomblé initiates)   132
*bori* (ritual of initiation)   131-2
bottles   136, 143, 147
bracelet   85, 112
Brazil   1-3, 16-19, 22-3, 25-7, 30-1, 35-7, 41, 45-6, 90-2, 97, 101-2, 114, 116, 124, 147
  northeast   31, 33
  regions   36, 144
Brazilian
  authorities   31, 148
  celebration   34
  cuisine   18, 33
  media stereotypes   145
  states   125
Brazilian military dictatorship   144

*búzios* (jogo de búzios)  2, 18, 50, 58, 114-16, 118, 123-5, 135

C

*cabeça* (head)  2, 100
*cabeça-feita*  36
Caboclo Candomblé  31
*caliph* (ruler of Islamic community)  21
*calundus*  19-20, 28-9
Candomblé  1-3, 9-10, 16, 25-6, 29-31, 33-6, 43, 45-7, 50, 53-7, 70-1, 132-7, 139-40, 143-4, 147-8
  ceremonies  20, 35, 106, 129, 131, 133
  communities  15, 28, 34, 85, 115, 125, 130, 132, 136, 139, 143
  culture of  1, 28, 30-1, 33, 50, 57, 106, 111, 148
  divinities  3, 6, 9, 15, 18, 30, 33, 35, 45, 79-80, 89-91, 101-2, 129-31, 135, 140-1
  feasts  76
  ground  31, 66, 70
  groups  19, 35
  kitchen  140
  knowledge  9-10, 18, 20, 57-8, 113, 116, 130, 132, 144, 149
  legends  85, 88-9, 101, 111
  liturgy  53, 67, 145
  origins of  1, 20, 27, 29, 144
  practitioners  35-6, 50, 57, 69, 97, 101, 136
  priest  6, 9, 27, 85, 115, 130-1, 144-5
  reclusion room  100, 139
  religious leaders  20, 34
  rituals  63, 136
  temples  1, 3, 9, 29-31, 36, 43, 45, 50, 55, 58, 114-15, 125, 129, 132-6, 139-41
  traditions  13, 23, 31, 36, 41, 50, 71, 100, 113, 117, 119, 125, 132, 143, 147-9
  transformed  147

Candomblés, of Bahia   115
captive individuals   5, 16-26, 30, 66, 116
Carioca Candomblé   3
carnival   34-5, 50, 144
casting (of cowrie shells)   113, 117-18, 125
Catholic Church   22-3, 26-7, 35
Catholic saints, images of   25, 27-8, 30-1, 80, 143
cemeteries   76, 85, 100, 102
character   115, 131
Christianity   19-20, 23, 111
cities   14, 17, 21-3, 27, 29, 34, 111, 137, 140
  ancient Yorùbá   14, 85
client   28, 125, 135
colors   3, 35, 41-2, 55, 62-3, 68, 70, 73, 77, 90, 92, 95, 112, 124, 143
  principal   83, 88
Congo   16, 31
consultation   112, 114-15, 124-5
corpses   102, 104
cowrie shells   80, 116, 123, 125
creation   6, 27, 41, 43, 48-50, 54, 62, 79, 113
Creator   41, 43, 47, 95, 148
Cuba   35, 49, 66, 77, 83, 86, 88, 90, 92, 97, 102, 124, 140
Cuban Candomblé   69
Cuban legends   99, 103
*curandeiros*   20
cycles (of migration)   17, 76

D

*dafa* (divination)   113, 117-18
dances   6, 26-8, 33, 37, 68, 83, 133, 149

INDEX

darkness  6, 104, 118
death  21, 75, 82, 85, 107, 137
devotees  2, 18, 136, 140
disguise  27-8, 31, 87
divination  18, 50, 53-4, 112-13, 115-16, 124, 132 *see also dafa*
divine forces  10
Dorival Caymmi  33-4, 148

E

earth  6, 14, 42-3, 47, 54, 56, 69-70, 75, 79, 81, 103-5, 113, 129-30, 134, 136-7
    sack of  49-50
*ebó* (offering)  3, 18, 35, 49-50, 56, 58, 61, 70, 80, 91, 125, 132, 134-6, 140
Egungun (Egun)  88, 105-7, 124
Elégua  61, 63 *see also* Exu
elements, natural  132
emancipation (freedom)  5, 20-1, 25-6, 30-1, 34
empires  21-2
enemies  19, 61, 87, 89
energy  43, 47-8, 55, 133, 136
*enredo*  131-2
*eré*  100
Europeans  16
Ewá  101-2, 124
Ewe-Fon  16, 18, 20
expansion  16, 41, 118
Exu  13, 35, 47, 49-50, 59, 61-3, 66, 100, 124, 135-6, 139-40

F

faith  7, 13, 23, 145
food  86, 134-6, 140, 148

forces of nature   5-6, 9-10, 18, 23-4, 41, 45-6, 56, 66, 113, 137
forests   25-6, 35, 45, 53, 66-8, 71-3, 135-6
Fulani   19

G

gender   10
Gil, Gilberto   34, 36, 148

H

head   2, 36, 46, 54, 86, 112, 130-2, 148 *see also cabeça*
healer-diviner   28-9
health   24, 50, 86, 89, 135
human beings   6, 10, 41-2, 46-7, 50, 70, 80, 95-6, 100, 133, 137, 141
hunters   53, 65, 67

I

Iansã   33-4, 53, 87
*iawo*   33, 129-30, 140, 144
Ìbejì   99
Iemanjá   34-5, 53-4, 91-2, 99, 102, 124
Ifá   18, 41, 48-50, 109, 111-15, 117-18, 124, 139
  consultation of   114, 117, 124-5, 130
  iroke   112-13
  priests of   54, 67, 80, 111-12, 115, 117
  tradition of   113-14, 117
*ikin*   112-13, 117, 124
Ile-Ife   14
illnesses   75-7
initiation   55, 58, 111-13, 116-17, 129, 131-2
  process of   111, 129, 131

Iroko (Orixá)   55, 69-70, 139
iron   42, 53, 65, 132
Islam   19-21, 111
*iwa-pelé*   41, 115 *see also* character
*iyalorixá* (priestess)   135, 140
*iyawo* (initiate)   100, 132-3
*iyerosun*   112-13

J

Jeje   1-2, 16-20, 23, 29, 45-6, 133
Jeje Candomblé   46-7, 63, 70
Jeje-Yorùbá pantheon   46

M

*malês* (Muslims)   19
matter   41-2, 48, 118, 144
messenger   43, 50, 61, 63, 80
Middle Ages   14-15
Middle East   20-1
Minkisi   9, 23, 148-9
miracles   9, 89-90, 148
Mohammed   21
music   34, 37, 134, 149
mysteries (of the Orixás)   9, 36, 75, 149
mythologies   13, 23, 25, 47-8, 50, 57, 62, 81, 86, 116, 140, 149

N

Nagô   16, 18, 45, 47
  tradition   49
Nanã Buruku   77, 81-2, 124

nations (nações)   16, 26-7
natural environments   53-4, 58, 91, 139
necklace   3, 77, 80
Nigeria   36, 103, 111
Nunes, Clara   33-4

O

Oba   86, 100-1, 112
Obàtálá   34, 36, 42, 48-9, 53-5, 69, 91, 95-7, 124
objects (sacred)   3, 132, 134-6, 143
ocean   34, 102-3
Ode-Remo   111
Odù   111, 116-19, 124-5
Odùduwà   49-50, 54, 101
Ogum   6, 13-14, 53-4, 65-6, 87, 111-12, 124
Okô   104
Olodumare   48
Olofi   47-9, 69
Olokun   91, 102-4
Olorun   48-50
Oluwo   112
Omiojuaro house of Candomblé   2
Omolu-Obaluiê   75-6, 87
*opelé-Ifá*   115-16, 124
Opon Ifá   112
Orishas   2-3, 10, 141 *see also* Orixás
Orixá of the head   58, 130, 132
Orixá religion   34, 53, 140 *see also* Candomblé
Orixás   2-3, 9-10, 33-4, 36, 45-50, 53-9, 61, 69-71, 75-6, 79-81, 99-103, 129-36, 139-40, 143-5, 147-9

honored  61, 65, 75, 85
Oshun  6, 34, 50, 53-4, 86, 89-90, 99-101
Oshunmare  77, 79-80, 124
Ossâim  35, 53-4, 68, 71-3, 81
*ota*  139
Oxóssi  34, 53-4, 56, 67-8, 124, 139
Oya  33, 53, 86-8, 102, 104, 107, 124
Oyo, kingdom of  16-17

P

palm nuts, sacred  112-13
Parés, Nicholas  1, 30
patron  65, 104
*peji*  139, 143, 147
plants  41, 46, 53, 55, 71, 79, 103, 130
Popular Brazilian Music  34-5
power  27, 43, 53, 71, 76, 80, 82, 87-8, 107, 130
prayers  54, 56, 58, 67, 113
prejudices  87-8, 144
priestesses  1, 129-31, 135, 148
priests  1, 55, 104, 129, 131, 135, 143, 147-8
processions  3, 6
purity  3, 95, 129

Q

Qur'an  19-21

R

rainbow  79-80
reason  13, 18, 61, 67, 81, 86

rebellion   22, 26
resistance   11, 111, 143-4, 147
resources, natural   72
rhythms   34-5, 130
Rio de Janeiro   2, 18, 22-3, 34-5, 37, 50, 66, 91
rituals   9, 18, 23, 25, 35, 42-3, 56-8, 63, 71, 100, 105, 107, 112, 129, 131-2
  principal   131-2
  public   30, 97, 100
rivers   26, 53, 55, 93, 100, 136
rosario (prayer beads)   124

S

Saci   35
sacrifices   18, 77, 86, 134, 137, 143
Saint Barbara   86, 88
Saint Geronimo   86
Salvador   13, 17, 19, 27, 29-31, 34-5, 37, 114-15, 144, 148
São Luis   17
sculptors   14-15
sea   6, 92, 136
serpent   79, 81
shrine   15, 43, 139-40
slavery   9, 13, 16-17, 20-2, 25-6, 28, 116
smallpox   75, 81, 87
society   28, 46, 107, 116, 133, 147
songs   33, 36, 56, 130, 133, 148-9
space, sacred   1, 30, 58, 65, 132, 140-1, 143, 147
Spiritualism   9, 129
stones, sacred   14, 42-3, 53, 55-6, 132, 139, 143
storms   54, 87, 89, 92

sun 47-9, 55, 103
supplicants 56, 67, 88, 92
symbolism 2, 36, 42, 57, 72, 79, 139, 149

T

Taoism 118
Togo 16-17, 36, 81, 86
trance 3, 20, 129-30, 134
trees 42, 55, 69-70, 113, 139, 148

U

Umbanda 31, 50, 76, 129, 135
universe 23, 48, 54, 118

V

*vatapá* 33
vegetables 58, 135-6
veneration 25, 27, 66, 68, 105, 107, 137, 145
Verger, Pierre 1, 3, 36, 119
Vodun religion 3, 9, 18, 23, 25, 30, 45-6, 133, 148-9

W

war 16, 18, 45, 48, 65-6, 87, 89
water 6, 43, 45, 54, 79-80, 91, 101, 103, 136, 139
wind 6, 53, 87
wisdom 15, 96, 113
women 5, 29, 41, 86, 88, 104-5

X

Xangô 6, 13, 34, 50, 53-4, 79, 85-7, 99-101, 124

Y

Yemanjá 34-5, 50, 53, 91
Yorùbá 3, 10, 13, 15-20, 23, 29, 41-2, 45, 47, 55, 81, 113, 115, 133, 140
  civilization 14-15, 54
  cosmogony 26, 45, 47
  divination 111
  divinities 13, 65
  kingdom 16, 18-19, 29
  language 10, 36, 134
  mythology 57, 91
  religion 1, 3, 41, 43, 106, 112-13
  society 13, 107

www.ingramcontent.com/pod-product-compliance
Lightning Source LLC
Chambersburg PA
CBHW052210090526
44584CB00019BA/2912